Fun, Festive & ★ Vegan ★ ⬦ous!
Holidays for Everyone

Recipes, Puns, Historic Lore and More
to Help You Celebrate Without Compromise

Marla Rose

Fun, Festive & Fabulous: Vegan Holidays for Everyone

Recipes, Puns, Historic Lore and More to Help You Celebrate Without Compromise

Marla Rose

with John Beske

To the billions of animals who have given me purpose and the millions of human animals who have given me hope. May we all celebrate true liberation one day.

To my grandparents, Nate and Dora: your love gave me everything I needed in life.

Table of Contents

Note: ★= new recipe developed for this book
(the rest are recipes we originally developed and posted on VeganStreet.com)

Drinks: Spiced Pumpkin Latté

Appetizers & Small Bites: Yummy Mummies; Pumpkin Cream Cheese Spread

Mains: Pumpkin Tamale Pie; Butternut Squash, Corn and Hominy Chili; Freaky Eyeball Pizza

Desserts: ★Chocolate Spiderwebs; ★Pumpkin Pudding; Pumpkin Chocolate Brownies; ★Peanut Butter Crispy Cups; ★Pumpkin Chocolate Chip Bread

Drinks: Apple Cider Slushies

Appetizers & Small Bites: Brussels Sprouts Sliders; Sweet Potato Bisque; ★Cornbread Muffins

Mains: The Whole Shebang Thanksgiving Roast; Savory Holiday Pie

Desserts: Thanksgiving Day Chocolate Bark; ★Easy Pumpkin Cheesecake Cookies

Me with Grandma Dora in 1981 (before my goth phase)

Why we need vegan holidays.

I remember my first holiday as a vegetarian well.
Let me set the stage…

The setting

Thanksgiving, circa mid-1980s, my family's dining room with extended family and friends. The china for special occasions is out and there is a dead turkey on a platter.

The central character

That would be me, wearing black head-to-toe, including my fingernail polish and big hair, matching my mood of general angst.

(Actually, the look pretty much described me at any juncture from 1981 – 1985, roughly, but the angst was especially heightened at Thanksgiving.)

I had become a vegetarian as a high school sophomore, fueled by just the vague but persistent notion that eating animals was not something I wanted to do anymore. Despite this not being an especially firm foundation, somehow, I stuck with it and the longer I did, the more I learned and the more I learned, the more I knew deep within myself that there was no going back. Despite the fact that I ate meat up until the day that I quit and, growing up, I salivated at just the thought of my grandmother's brisket, going vegetarian felt like what I had to do. I had no way of knowing that this vague inkling would influence the purpose and trajectory of my life so powerfully and lay the groundwork for my eventual veganism, something I have dedicated my life to promoting. On that Thanksgiving Day in the mid-1980s, though, I was pretty annoyed and not just because our neighbor, Mrs. Brown, kept talking to me about what she saw as my looming protein deficiency (she was a dentist's wife, she kept reminding me) and that I was stuck at the kiddie table. Again.

As the only vegetarian, I felt like there was a hot spotlight on me and I just wanted the meal to be over. I was feeling self-conscious, annoyed and resentful. The turkey's corpse was turning into a skeleton with each new slice from it and I was feeling queasy and depressed. I was told to "eat around" the meat, which was in the gravy, the stuffing and possibly even in the pumpkin pie for all I knew. (Yes, in hindsight, I should have figured out how to cook myself something.) (Hindsight is 20/20, you know.) (There probably wasn't actually meat in the pumpkin pie. I mean, it was bad but not that bad.)

Thankfully, I am both stubborn and defiant by nature so despite that less than auspicious first holiday experience, I stuck with my vegetarianism and, slowly but surely, things seemed to get a little better every year. One turning point was in college, when I got an apartment with a tiny kitchen and gingerly started branching out from making Stove Top Stuffing for every dinner. As I learned how to cook a little, familiar but dormant memories were awakened within me of how much I loved to spend time in the kitchen with my much-adored grandmother as a child. I started buying vegetarian cookbooks at the local used bookstore. I started figuring out which recipes sounded the best me. I started learning how to adapt them to my preferences. Cooking became more intuitive and my many kitchen flops helped me to learn more. (It turns out three bulbs of garlic is not the same thing as three cloves and should be avoided unless you want your Gado Gado to the most garlicky ever. You're welcome.) I started making dishes other people could enjoy. I started learning which world cuisines had the most options for vegetarians and how to order at restaurants. As a vegetarian and eventual vegan, things slowly started getting better, except the holidays pretty much sucked for a while.

Act two

A second major turning point for me was being invited to be a part of an annual Thanksgiving meal tradition, a vegan one, with friends in the mid-1990s. This time, I was a new vegan. It was *ah-may-zing*. From that day on, my attitude about Thanksgiving shifted 180 degrees: it became something I actually eagerly anticipated instead of actively dreaded. There were colorful salads, hearty casseroles, savory meatless "turkeys," exquisite pumpkin cheesecakes and much more, all made without a stitch of animal products; there was magic in the air and not just from those intoxicating aromas. This new Thanksgiving tradition still felt like a holiday – but much better – and it helped me to really internalize that plant-based diets are not about deprivation but abundance, not about restriction but conscious choice. Even more appealing than the unforgettable food was the camaraderie of people sitting down to eat together, to laugh, talk, conspire and enjoy the company of one another without a dead animal anywhere in sight. That spirit of inclusion and belonging reminded me again of my grandparents and their holiday gatherings with my extended family, raucous, warm and joyful meals made all the more wonderful for the company. It occurred to me that our vegan Thanksgiving meal felt like we were actively transforming this holiday, which is so full of suffering and pain, into something entirely different. It was revelatory.

Thanksgiving was the holiday that was my gateway into transforming celebrations through a vegan lens and now it includes most of them, even those I don't celebrate otherwise. From Christmas to Passover, Fourth of July – to my personal favorite – Halloween, there is no reason why vegans can't celebrate with verve and every reason why we should. Transforming holidays through a vegan sensibility is creative but can also help us to reconnect to traditions we love but may have left behind for a multitude of reasons. Participating in this way can help us to feel connected and nostalgic, yes, but also pioneering as we offer an example of engaging in the world with a compassionate, inclusive and joyful vegan sensibility.

That's why I created this ebook and what I hope to offer people: a point of entry to different celebrations that can be enjoyed without harming or being complicit in needless cruelty to other animals. Enjoyment is empathized because with celebrating the holidays, it is not about what we are avoiding but the exciting and delicious ways of participating that don't require a compromise.

Back at my first Thanksgiving as a vegetarian, eager as I was for it to be over, little could I have imagined the world we'd inhabit now as vegans, one with robust communities around the world, ample food options abounding, and new adherents and innovations every day. What has been behind this transformation? Many things, not the least of which is sitting down together as conscious creators. Veganism is about abundance, justice and extending the circle of compassion to include those unfairly relegated to the outside. We are creating a new world. As we are seeing from household to household all around the globe, more and more people realize that this is something wonderful to celebrate.

Let's enjoy…

XO -

MarlaRose

Vegan Holiday food philosophy

All of my recipes are going to be vegan (say what?!) but they are also gluten-free because of my sensitivity to gluten, which is found in wheat (and its derivatives, like semolina and spelt), barley, rye and some other foods. I can't develop a recipe if I can't taste it, thus the recipes in this trusty e-book are vegan and gluten-free. (If you are not gluten-free yourself, well, thank your lucky stars and feel free to substitute regular flour, seitan for tofu, etc.) Please note that while I am gluten-free, I harbor no ill-will (except envy) toward gluten-eaters and understand that it is among the foods that most vegans can enjoy.

Speaking of, there does seem to be a trend of vegans who don't eat sugar, oil, nuts, fat, nightshades, salt, etc. This is their, and perhaps your, prerogative. Those items, while vegan, do not align with everyone's dietary approach or wellness goals. I do use some of those ingredients, usually sparingly, in some of these recipes, though not all. My recipes were created with the attitude that especially with celebrations, people like to splurge a little and enjoy foods that are reminiscent of what they may have enjoyed as pre-vegans. If we remove items that can enhance flavor – like salt and fat – it can be less like what we once enjoyed and taste more like "restrictive" food. Whatever you choose for your dietary philosophy is up to you but my goal was to create vegan recipes that are easy to make, inexpensive and delicious, emphasizing of whole plant ingredients that are easy to source, and, with the exception of gluten, not restrictive.

On some of the recipes, you will notice **Dial it Down**, **Dial it Up** or **Glam it Up** graphics. This gives you ideas for increasing or decreasing decadence as you wish. Customization is key to enjoyment at times and can help you to make recipes that are just right for you.

dial it **Down**

dial it **Up**

Glam it up

How to be the hostess with the mostest.

One of the biggest worries people reading this may have with regard to holidays is they fear that hosting a meal and "imposing" vegan food on guests may come off as rude and unwelcoming. I will concur that while many people have some deeply entrenched notions about food and custom, we can still celebrate without compromise and strive to be inclusive of everyone despite holding some very different views and practices.

Vegan Potlucks
building a healthier and friendlier world one meal at a time.
VeganStreet.com
patreon.com/veganstreet

To me, successful vegan hosting really comes down to clarity and friendliness. If you are hosting, being clear and confident that it is your prerogative to maintain the standards of your home is key to getting over roadblocks. Just as you wouldn't be expected to serve non-kosher food to accommodate guests if you maintained a kosher home, nor should you be expected to drop your vegan standards to accommodate non-vegan guests in your home. Remind yourself: it is just one meal. Also remember that while people will do what they want to do outside of your home, you have every right to determine the parameters of what happens in your home. In other words, your home, your rules.

That said, there are ways to be inclusive while maintaining your vegan standards. Here is what I recommend:

• Be honest. If someone asks if your event is going to be vegan, don't hem and haw or be vague with your response. Just keep it to the exact subject – don't say, "Yes, of course if I host it's going to be vegan because I am not a heartless monster who allows people to feast on the corpses of innocent beings in my home!" – and keep it succinct.

- Aim to accommodate less adventurous palates unless you know otherwise. Create recipes that are familiar to the holiday and have had good reviews. Query your vegan foodie friends for some of their favorite crowd-pleasing recipes. Your meat-and-potatoes uncle is probably not going to be impressed by your nutritional yeast-and-rejuvelac sauce over tempeh so save that for a vegan potluck. (Or yourself.)

- Emphasize the spirit of the holiday, not the ways in which your celebration will be different. You will have great food and company: is there really anything more than you need? Decorate, have fun, get tipsy!

- Stay positive. It is not the time for discussing the horrors of the dairy industry, for example. If anyone wants to talk about this, tell him or her that you are happy to discuss, just not at your celebration.

- Reassure if necessary. I know that it's annoying, but there are some people who really need to be coddled to avoid meltdowns. If someone is really concerned that not having Grandma Betty's turducken is really going to ruin Thanksgiving or that they will be eating nothing but sprouts and raw turnips, nip it in the bud with the confident reassurance that your meal together will be lovely and delicious.

- If someone wants to bring vegan food, let 'em! If they need help, share some dependable recipes with them. This is a great way to include others in the process.

- If someone wants to bring non-vegan food and you are not okay with this, don't be okay with it. How you handle being "not okay" is up to you but to me, it means speaking honestly that I don't serve dead animals in my home. I communicate that I'd still love the person's company, though.

How to get your vegan on at someone else's party

While hosting a celebration has its unique challenges (how many times can you tell your cousin to PLEASE not bring her authentic Swedish meatballs to your party before you're ready to call in the National Guard?), at the very least, you call the shots because you are hosting. When you are attending someone else's soirée, in some ways you are at the mercy of the host. By this I mean you are less in control and I know that this requires a bit of trust.

Given that, here are your options:

A. You can refuse to attend.

B. You can attend but shoot the evil eye at people as you hunker down in the corner with a plate of celery.

C. You can contact the host and ask if you can bring vegan food. This opens up the conversation for the host to say yes or no. If your host says yes, ask what you can bring. What I recommend is bringing something that offers plenty of portions to share. (Yes, I'm an overcompensating Type A person and you don't need to be like me. Yes, I'd bring dessert, too.) If your host says no, you don't need to bring anything, there will be plenty of food for you, ask if there is anything you can do to make things easier. Keep the lines of communication open to minimize misunderstandings.

I choose option C. We want to demonstrate to the world that veganism isn't about sacrifice and exclusion, right? If we engage, especially while in possession of beautiful and tantalizing food, we are helping to change people's opinions about veganism and vegan food. If it's too upsetting to be around dead animals, though, that is certainly understandable and your choice to make.

Halloween

I will admit it: I am an unrepentant Halloween fiend. As someone who has always had an affinity for the old, creaky and slightly creepy – growing up, I would have moved into The Addams Family manor no questions asked and Morticia was my style icon – and I still love the brisk temperatures as well as the creativity, the quirkiness and the spooky, spirited fun of the season. Here you will find recipes to help to get you in the mood for a festive and fabulous Halloween.

Why did Dracula stop eating meat?

He had a bad experience with a stake.

Why did the Bride of Dracula have insomnia?

His coffin was driving her nuts.

Drinks
Spiced Pumpkin Latte

Don't want to spend a bunch of money on a fancy coffee drink? Here's a recipe to make it right at home. It's a lot less expensive and you can tailor it just to your tastes.

1 cup brewed coffee
½ cup non-dairy milk (a flavored vegan nog would work, too)
2 tablespoons pumpkin purée
2 tablespoons maple syrup or sweetener of choice
1 teaspoon pure vanilla extract
½ teaspoon pumpkin pie spice blend
1 – 2 tablespoons vegan whipped topping

In a medium saucepan, heat the coffee, milk, pumpkin purée, sweetener, vanilla and spice blend. Whisk to remove any lumps.

Pour into a cup and top with vegan whipped topping or enjoy without.

Didja Know?
Halloween has its origins in the ancient Celtic pagan tradition of Samhain, pronounced "sow-in" (as in cow-in), which celebrated the end of the harvest year and marked the beginning of winter and the period ahead of darkness. Samhain was considered a transitional time, when the boundary between life on earth and the spirit world was the most permeable.

Yummy Mummies

Like a pizza on an English muffin canvas, Yummy Mummies were something I engineered years ago for our Chicago Vegan Family Network potlucks and ever since, it's not a real Halloween party unless we have them. Simple, fun, and tasty, children love these.

6 English muffins
12 tablespoons tomato-basil marinara
24 sliced olive "eyes"
48 thin strips of vegan cheese

Preheat the oven to 375 degrees. Split the English muffins in half so you have 12 halves. Spread approximately 1 tablespoon of marinara on each half. Lay four strips of cheese across the English muffins at different angles so they look like mummy wrapping. Place two olive slices on each "mummy" for eyes. Place the mummies on a parchment lined or lightly oiled cookie sheet. Bake for about 14 - 16 minutes, or until the cheese is beginning to melt.

Why did everyone always get the better of Dracula?

Because he was such a sucker.

What is the werewolf's favorite leafy green?

Aruuuu-gula.

PUMPKIN CREAM CHEESE SPREAD

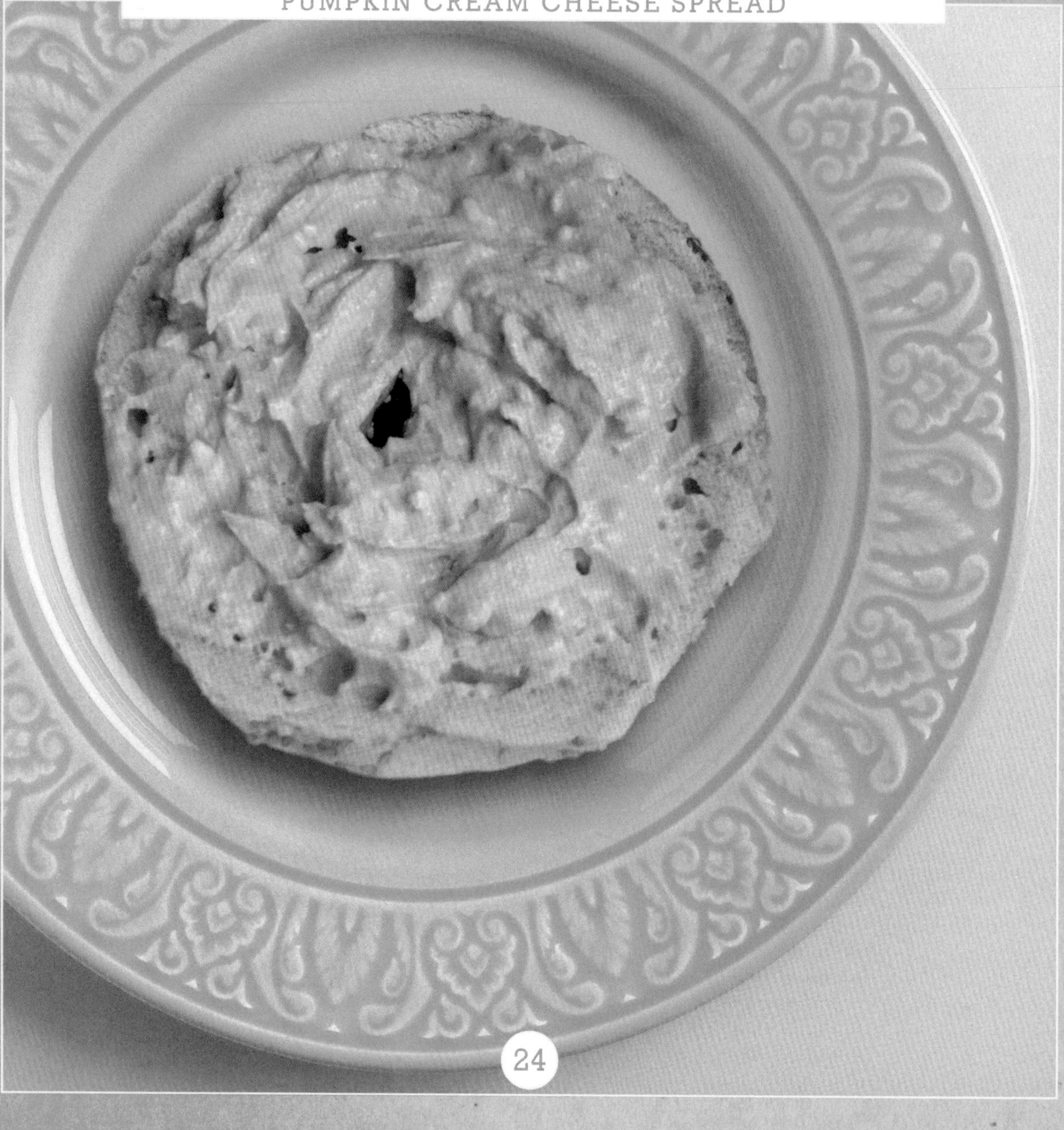

Pumpkin Cream Cheese Spread

This spread works great on bagels, tortilla roll-ups or even spread on apples. Pumpkin-y and rich without being cloyingly sweet, this will make any autumn enthusiast swoon.

8-oz. vegan cream cheese, room temperature
½ cup plus 2 tablespoons pumpkin purée (not pumpkin pie mix)
2 tablespoons real maple syrup
1 teaspoon pure vanilla extract
½ teaspoon pumpkin pie spice blend (optional)

In a medium bowl, mix all ingredients together until smooth. You can also use a stand mixer or food processor to mix. Mix thoroughly and serve. This is great chilled.

Didja Know?

Originally, jack-o'-lanterns were carved out of turnips and potatoes in Ireland and it wasn't until Irish immigrated into North America, where pumpkins are native and abundant, that the orange gourd replaced root vegetables as the illuminated symbols of Halloween in the 19th and 20th centuries. Jack-o'-lanterns have their origins in an Irish folktale where a character named Stingy Jack, in trouble with the devil for his shenanigans, must wander the earth for eternity with a lighted coal in a carved-out turnip. Adopted for All Hallows' Eve, these lanterns were also thought to scare away roaming spirits.

Pumpkin Tamale Pie

Put together the comfort of tamales with the earthy flavors of autumn produce, and you have a warming, cozy dish that is just impressive enough to serve guests without all the labor of tamales. Pumpkin adds great, fat-free, beta-carotene rich moisture to the masa dough crust while not being too assertive with its flavor. This Pumpkin Tamale Pie is naturally gluten-free and can be modified to add anything you'd like inside the filling: more hot peppers (or none at all), kale in the place of Swiss chard, dairy-free cheese, and so on, but I liked this just as it was. While it takes a little more effort than most of the recipes in this book, it's still easy for a novice and I think it's one of those dishes you will still want to make over and over. This is perfect potluck food, too. You can find masa harina - made from hominy - in the Latin section of most grocery stores.

Tamale crust:
2 cups masa harina
1 teaspoon baking powder
½ teaspoon salt
1 tablespoon olive oil (optional)
½ cup pumpkin purée
2 cups low sodium vegetable broth, warm

Pie Filling:
1 large yellow onion, diced
4 tablespoons broth, divided
2 teaspoon cumin
1 teaspoon oregano

Which apples are always ready for a party?

Galas

27

Pumpkin Tamale Pie (cont.)

1 - 2 teaspoons chili powder
½ teaspoon cinnamon
Salt, pepper and hot pepper flakes
(to taste)
3 - 4 cloves garlic, minced
1 - 2 jalapeños, minced and seeds
removed to your preference
(more seeds will make it hotter)
1 medium butternut squash,
peeled and diced, seeds removed
2 tablespoons tamari
1 bunch Swiss chard, cut
into ribbons
3 cups cooked aduki or black
beans, drained and rinsed
1 lime

Preheat your oven to 350 degrees. Find a 8-inch square pan and a larger rectangular pan, like 9-x-13. Fill the large pan with about two inches of water and put that in the oven to warm up. Grease the square pan.

In a medium bowl, combine the masa harina, baking powder and salt. In a small bowl (I used a glass measuring cup), add a small amount of warm stock to the pumpkin and stir to integrate. Add the optional olive oil, the rest of the stock and stir to combine. Pour this into the masa dough, mixing with a large spoon or a whisk until fully combined. The dough should be soft.

Heat a large skillet over medium-high heat; add two tablespoons of broth. Let this heat for a minute, then add the onion and spices, stirring for three - four minutes. Add the garlic and jalapeño pepper and sauté for about five minutes. Add the butternut squash cubes, tamari and two tablespoons of broth. Cook until the butternut squash is easily pierced with a fork but is not mushy, about 12 - 14 minutes. (Stir frequently to prevent sticking!) Add the Swiss chard (you may need to do this in stages in order for it to all fit in your pan) and beans until the chard is wilted, a few minutes. Turn off the heat and squeeze a lime on top, stirring through.

Divide the masa dough in half. Put half on the bottom of the square pan and press it in. Add the filling to the pan, pushing down with the flat side of the spatula to make it flat on top. Press the rest of the masa dough on top and cover tightly with foil

Put this pan in the larger pan with water that is now hot (be careful!). Bake for 45 minutes. Remove from the oven and let it cool for 10 - 15 minutes, Cut into squares and sprinkle on optional toasted pumpkin seeds (put these in the oven in a pie plate for the last 7 minutes of baking the tamale pie, shaking half way); garnish with dairy-free sour cream, hot sauce, salsa and more.

Didja Know?

Our tradition today of dressing up for Halloween originated from the tradition of townspeople disguising themselves as demons and spirits in order to escape the notice of the real spirits wandering the streets during Samhain, thought to be wandering the earth due to the thin boundary between the living and the dead on Oct. 31. Offerings – treats – were left out to distract and appease the spirits.

Butternut Squash, Corn & Hominy Chili

With naturally sweet butternut squash and corn complemented by the spicy chiles, chewy hominy and beans in a smoky tomato sauce, this chili shows once again that even with just plant ingredients, we can still have a complex, satisfying dish that fills us up without slowing us down. Serve on quinoa or rice with avocado or dairy-free sour cream. (Or both!)

(By the way, I like a very thick chili: if you prefer it more soupy, simply add more vegetable stock.)

1²⁄₃ cups low-sodium vegetable stock, divided (more if you prefer a thinner chili).
1 yellow onion, diced
3 - 5 cloves garlic, minced
1 jalapeño, seeded and minced, (optional)*
1 poblano pepper, seeded and minced, (optional)
½ butternut squash, peeled, seeds removed and cut into smallish, uniform squares
1 tablespoon tamari
1 tablespoon dried basil

1 teaspoon dried thyme
¼ - ½ teaspoon ground cinnamon
¼ - ½ teaspoon cayenne powder
½ tablespoon or more chili powder
2 cups defrosted organic corn
30 oz. black beans, rinsed and drained
28-oz. crushed tomatoes
25-ounces hominy, drained and rinsed
1 - 2 tablespoons adobo sauce, (optional)**
Salt and pepper to taste

In a large, deep skillet (cast iron is perfect for this if you have one), heat ⅓ cup of vegetable stock over medium heat. Add the onion, and sauté, stirring often, for about six minutes. Add the garlic, peppers, butternut squash, additional ⅓ cup of vegetable stock, tamari and spices. Raise the temperature to medium-high, and cook, stirring often, for 10 - 13 minutes, until the squash pieces are softened.

Add the corn, black beans, crushed tomatoes, hominy and adobo sauce as well as final 1 cup of vegetable stock. Simmer on medium-low heat for 15 - 20 minutes. Enjoy over grains or potatoes with optional toppings. To serve in bell peppers, cut out a pumpkin face with a sharp knife (or don't), remove seeds and membrane and bake, standing up, in a pan at 375 degrees for 30 - 40 minutes or until the pepper is appropriately decrepit looking. Look for peppers with flattish bottoms for this.

*Use whatever peppers you like, these were the ones I chose.

**You can find chipotle peppers packed in adobo sauce in the Latino section of most well-stocked grocery stores. The sauce is unnecessary to this recipe but lends an enticing smoky flavor.

Freaky Eyeball Pizza

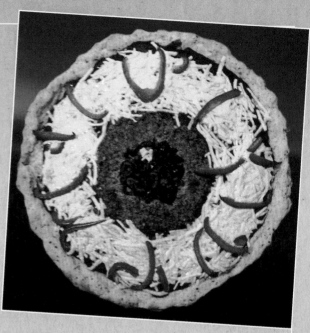

The elegantly named *Freaky Eyeball Pizza* is a really pretty simple combination of complementary flavors: vegan mozzarella, pizza sauce, pesto (seriously, this is a damn good pesto for people who are trying to limit oil, which is kind of silly to use on a pizza with cheese but still, you could use it again for other things) red peppers and olives. Feel free to use the items you'd like to create the classic gaping eyeball. Another idea is to make a Mexican-style pizza with guacamole for the iris and black beans for the pupil. The other thing that makes this a fun dish to make is if you are in the mood for something easy, most of these items are or could be purchased pre-made.

Enough dough for one 16-inch pizza (I used Bob's Red Mill Gluten-free Multigrain Pizza Crust Mix)*
1½ - 2 cups pizza sauce
About 2 cups vegan mozzarella shreds
Pesto (recipe on the next page)
⅓ – ½ cup chopped olives
½ red bell pepper, cut into thin slices

32

Prepare and pre-bake your pizza crust according to package instructions.

Spread pizza sauce across the crust using the back of a large spoon or a silicon spatula. Leave about 1 – 2 inches of space at the edge.

In the middle, scoop your pesto. Cover part of that in a ring of mozzarella like the white part of the eye. On top of that, mound a little circle of chopped olives. My husband thought to put a little mozzarella in that, too, like the glinting in an eye. Place some red bell pepper slices across the surface like blood vessels.

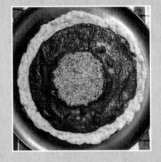

Pesto recipe:

2 cups fresh basil
2 cups spinach
½ cup toasted walnuts or pine nuts
¼ cup low-sodium vegetable broth
2 teaspoons mild white miso paste
2 teaspoons fresh lemon juice
1 teaspoon organic lemon peel, grated
Salt and pepper to taste

Purée in a food processor until combined.

(By the way, this will make more than you need for this recipe so enjoy in other uses as well.)

* You could also use a ready-made crust.

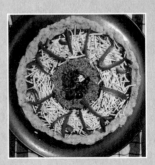

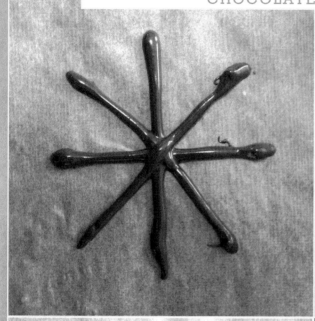

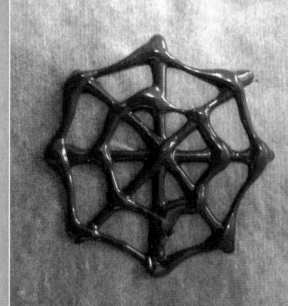

Chocolate Spiderwebs

You can make chocolate spiderwebs – or other designs! – with just some melted chocolate, parchment paper, a cookie sheet and just a little time in the 'fridge. I freehand draw the simple chocolate designs I make but you can also print out designs and trace them onto parchment paper with a marker: just flip the parchment paper over and trace that when you actually "draw" with chocolate. Properly melting chocolate so it is glossy, has a nice snap and doesn't have streaks requires a couple of simple tempering steps any home cook can do in the steps I have outlined below.

½ tablespoon refined coconut oil or vegan butter
6 oz. slavery-free, vegan chocolate chips (see page 43)

Line your cookie sheet with a piece of parchment paper. If you are tracing the design, have this drawn on and turned over.

Fill a medium pot about ¼ full with water. Bring to a boil. Reduce the heat to simmer and fit a larger bowl, ideally glass or metal, over the top of the pot, making sure that it doesn't touch the water and that it is a tight fit without gaps. Add the chocolate chips, reserving ¼ cup, stirring frequently until melted. Carefully remove the bowl from the top of the pot without turning off the burner and add the reserved chocolate chips, stirring until melted. Return to heat and stir often until it is warmed through. Turn off the heat.

Place your melted chocolate in a squeeze bottle. I made my spiderwebs with by making a lowercase "t" and then intersecting the middle with two diagonal lines. From there, I connected the lines with chocolate. Shake your squeeze bottle over a bowl to get the chocolate to the bottom and avoid air pockets.

Once you have your designs all drawn out, place flat in the fridge on your cookie sheet until solid, about an hour.

Pumpkin Pudding

There is not much that is more comforting than homemade pudding, especially one as rich, creamy and homey as this one. This easy, tasty dish evokes all the warm feelings of autumn in pudding form.

1 ½ cups dairy-free milk
½ cup cashews, soaked in water for at least an hour and drained
1 cup pureed pumpkin (not pumpkin pie filling)
⅓ cup plus two tablespoons pure maple syrup
2 teaspoons pure vanilla extract
1 teaspoon ground cinnamon
½ teaspoon ground ginger
½ teaspoon ground nutmeg
4 tablespoons cornstarch
Pinch of salt

Blend together the non-dairy milk and cashews for 30 seconds or until smooth. Add the pumpkin, maple syrup, vanilla, cinnamon, ginger and nutmeg to the blender and blend until smooth. Add to a medium pot along with the cornstarch and pinch of salt; cook over medium-low heat, whisking frequently, until thickened, five to six minutes. Transfer into serving cups, cover, and cool for at least an hour before serving.

 dial it **Down**

Just use milk without the cashews. It will be less rich but that is what you want, right?

 dial it **Up**

Use a holiday nog-type milk..

Dollop with vegan whipped topping.

Garnish the glass with a spooky chocolate treat. See page 35

Pumpkin Chocolate Brownies

I believe in the occasional treat and to me, a brownie is the perfect treat. While I like treats, I also like to have them be as close to healthy as I can without them being some mashed-up dates and walnuts pretending to be brownies.

These are treats without added oil. I used that old standby of applesauce to stand in for fat, and the puréed pumpkin does that job nicely itself. (By the way, if you don't like pumpkin or you don't have it on hand, puréed sweet potato is the ideal 1-for-1 substitute.) The result is a moist, fudge-y brownie, my very favorite kind, with just a whisper of pumpkin. I hope you love these as much as we do.

1 tablespoon flax seed, ground
3 tablespoons water
1¼ cup gluten-free all-purpose flour (I used Bob's Red Mill 1-to-1 Baking Flour)
½ cup slavery-free cocoa powder (see page 43)
2 tablespoons arrowroot
2 teaspoons baking powder
½ teaspoon cinnamon

¼ **teaspoon nutmeg**
¼ **teaspoon salt**
⅓ **slavery-free chocolate chips, plus 1 - 2 tablespoons for the top**
(see page 43)
1 cup pumpkin puree
½ **cup maple syrup**
¼ **cup applesauce**
1 tablespoon pure vanilla extract

Preheat your oven to 325 degrees. Grease or line a 8-X-8-inch baking pan.

In a small cup or bowl, combine the flax and water, whisking or mixing with a fork together. Store this in the fridge for at least 15 minutes.

In a large bowl, sift or whisk the flour, cocoa powder, arrowroot, baking soda, cinnamon, nutmeg and salt. Mix in the ⅓ cup of chocolate chips.

In a medium bowl, stir or whisk together the pumpkin purée, maple syrup, applesauce, vanilla and chilled flax "goop." Pour into the flour mix and stir until incorporated. It will be thick but soft.

Pour into the prepared pan and press the reserved chocolate chips into the top.

Bake for 20 minutes, turn 180 degrees, then bake for 13 more minutes. Let cool for 20 - 30 minutes and enjoy!

Didja Know?
The very first Peanuts special in which Lucy pulls the football away from an all-too-trusting Charlie Brown was in 1966's *It's the Great Pumpkin, Charlie Brown*.

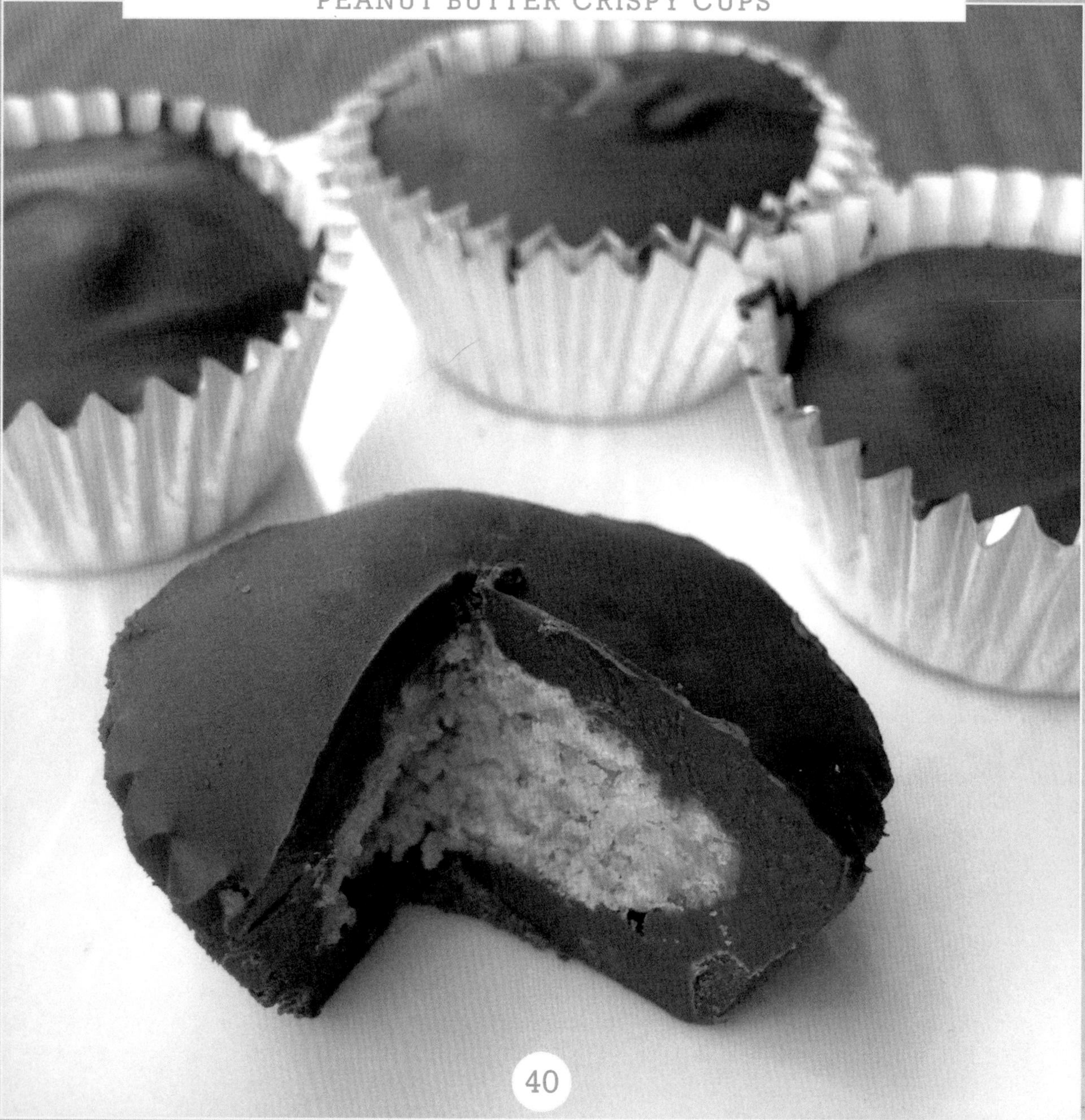

Peanut Butter Crispy Cups

True story: when I was in middle school, I was cast as Gollum at my overnight camp's production of The Hobbit. I loved the role that was tailor-made for a shameless scenery chewer such as yours truly but I didn't love the Rice Krispy treats I needed to voraciously gobble in a scene. For years afterwards, I steadfastly avoided Rice Krispy treats until I tried them again as an adult, ones that were a little more mature than the sticky-sweet ones I remember from childhood. It turns out that peanut butter helps to mellow the sharp sweetness and chocolate, well, chocolate is everything. These treats are like a mash-up between a peanut butter cup and a crispy treat. I recommend using refined coconut oil in this if you don't use butter; unrefined coconut oil will have a coconut-y flavor that you might not enjoy. I like coconut myself just fine, though!

1 tablespoon refined coconut oil or vegan butter
12 oz. slavery-free, vegan chocolate chips, reserving ¼ cup (see page 43)
1 tablespoon coconut oil or vegan butter
5 oz. vegan marshmallows
¼ cup peanut butter or nut butter of preference
1 teaspoon pure vanilla extract
2 cups crisp rice cereal
1 teaspoon maca powder (optional)
Pinch of salt (not needed if using salted nut butter)

Line a mini-muffin pan with 12 liners.

Fill a medium pot about ¼ full with water. Bring to a boil. Reduce the heat to simmer and fit a larger bowl, ideally glass or metal, over the top pot, making sure that it doesn't touch the water and that it is a tight fit without gaps. Add the chocolate, reserving the ¼ cup, stirring frequently until melted. Carefully

Peanut Butter Crispy Cups (cont.)

remove the bowl from the top of the pot without turning off the burner and add the reserved chocolate chips, stirring until melted.

Return to heat and stir often until it is warmed through. Turn off the heat.

Using a small spoon, add about ½ tablespoon of melted chocolate to the bottom and a little up the sides of each liner. The back of the spoon works great on this and don't worry about it looking perfect. This will be the bottom of each cup. When all liners have the bottom layer of chocolate in them, store in the refrigerator for 20 minutes.

Meanwhile, make your crispy centers.

Heat the coconut oil or butter over medium-low heat in a medium pan. Add the marshmallows and stir with a large spoon until melted. Add the nut butter, vanilla, maca powder and salt into a medium pan and stir until thick, goopy and uniform. Add the rice crispy cereal by the half-cup until incorporated, stirring until combined. Don't worry if some crispies get mashed. It will be thick and crumbly and but it should stick together if mushed with your fingers.

Removed the cooled chocolate-lined cups from the fridge. Add a little less than a teaspoon or so of crispy filling in the center of each cup. Roll it with your hands and fingers to shape it. Top with the rest of the melted chocolate until covered. Refrigerate until cool, about an hour.

Note:

You should have lots of rice crispy filling left over from your Peanut Butter Crispy Cups. Here's what you can do: add a couple more tablespoons of peanut butter and a tablespoon of vegan butter or coconut oil to a small pot along with the leftover crispies over medium-low heat. Stir until dry and mixed together. Pat the crispies into a lightly-oiled loaf pan and refrigerate until cool and firm.

The Dark Side of Chocolate

Unfortunately, there is a bitter - though often hidden - side to the chocolate industry, which is that cacao (a.k.a. cocoa) is harvested using child-labor in most West African-sourced chocolate products, which accounts for more than 70% of the world's cocoa supply. The labor, often trafficked, illegal and forced, is brutal, cruelly long, dangerous, abusive and exploitative of some of the world's most impoverished and vulnerable people. It is approximated that nearly two million children in the Ivory Coast and Ghana alone labor under the brutal practices of the cocoa industry while candy manufacturers like Mars, Hershey and Nestlé look the other way and keep reaping profits off their suffering.

Often, people assume that vegan chocolate - meaning chocolate that is made without milk products - is cruelty-free but that is not always the case. The best way to ensure that your dollars do not support child slavery is to check out the free Chocolate List from the Food Empowerment Project (available in iPhone and Android) so you can check it every time you buy chocolate. The list is also available for viewing at **foodispower.org/chocolate-list**

Pumpkin-Chocolate Chip Bread

Is there much that is more delicious and evocative of autumn than fresh pumpkin bread? As soon as we decided to do this e-book, the first previously unpublished recipe I knew that I wanted to include was pumpkin bread. This pumpkin bread, rich but not too sweet with a nice crumb, came to me as a vision and that vision included chocolate chips. Who am I to deny a vision? If chocolate chips aren't your thing, consider toasted nuts (pecans would be great or maybe toasted pepitas on top) but the chocolate adds a rich, gooey decadence to this wholesome loaf.

Flax egg
1 tablespoon ground flax seeds
3 tablespoons aquafaba or water (p 107)

Dry ingredients
2 cups all-purpose, gluten-free flour blend (I used Bob's Red Mill 1-for-1 Baking Flour)
1½ teaspoons ground cinnamon
½ teaspoon ground ginger
¼ teaspoon ground nutmeg
¼ teaspoon ground cardamom
1½ teaspoons baking powder
1 teaspoon baking soda
½ teaspoon xanthan gum
½ teaspoon salt

Wet ingredients
1 cup pureed pumpkin (not pumpkin pie mix)
¼ cup neutral oil (I used refined coconut oil)
½ cup pure maple syrup
1 teaspoon pure vanilla extract
¼ cup unsweetened applesauce
½ cup dairy-free sour cream, homemade or store bought

⅔ cup slavery-free chocolate chips, reserving a tablespoon for pressing on the top (see page 43)

Preheat your over to 350 degrees. Line a 9-inch loaf pan with parchment paper.

In a small cup, combine the ground flax and aquafaba or water. A mini-whisk is perfect for stirring together but a spoon or fork works fine as well. Put in the fridge as you prepare everything else.

In a large bowl, combine the dry ingredients and whisk together until combined.

In a medium bowl or large measuring cup, combine the wet ingredients, including the flax mixture.

Pour the pumpkin mixture into the dry mixture and stir together with a large spoon or silicone scraper/spatula until mostly combined. Mix in your chocolate chips, reserving a tablespoon, and stir until combined.

Pour into your prepared loaf pan, flatten the top until smooth, and sprinkle on the reserved chocolate chips, gently pressing in.

Bake for 23 minutes, turn 180 degrees, and bake 23 more minutes or until a toothpick inserted into the middle comes out clean. Cool in pan for 15 minutes, remove, and finish cooling on a cooling rack. Slice and serve when completely cooled.

 dial it **D**own

Replace all the oil in the original recipe with applesauce (so ½ cup altogether instead of ¼ cup). Keep in mind that most commercial vegan sour cream has oil in it so if you want to avoid oil altogether, make a homemade sour cream.

 dial it **U**p

Toast a slice and smear with vegan cream cheese! Ooo la la! Perfect for a fall morning.

Might I Recommend a Turkey-Free Thanksgiving?

VeganStreet.com

Thanksgiving

As I wrote in the introduction, Thanksgiving was my gateway to celebrating holidays as a vegan and it remains one of the most intoxicating days of the calendar year for me. Not everyone celebrates Thanksgiving with just other vegans but no matter how your meal comes together, enjoying delicious, gorgeous and warmly appreciated vegan food is a powerful antidote to the cruelties – against humans and other animals – associated with the holiday.

Why was the pumpkin pie irritated in the crowded 'fridge?

It was squashed.

A tortured dead bird with dried bread stuffed into its anal cavity is a symbol of gratitude and abundance.

(And vegans are the crazy ones...)

Drinks
Apple Cider Slushies

Is this two-ingredient, one-step recipe too easy? Yes. No. Sort of. I have no idea. The fact is, I saw a mention of apple cider slushies at a pumpkin patch we were at and thought, wow, that sounds tasty. I promptly made one at home and they are tasty. Got a freezer? Got a blender? Then you can make some yourself.

2 cups cold or room temperature apple cider
2 cups ice

Add both to the blender and pulse or blend under the ice has been slushified.

Didja Know?

According to late vegetarian historian Rynn Berry, at the original Thanksgiving, "The main meal was a sort of corn meal mush along with nuts and fruits such as gooseberries, strawberries, plums, cherries, cranberries and a groundnut known as the bogg bean. Popcorn and popcorn balls made by the Indians with maple syrup were served as a sweet. There was a variety of breadstuffs such as cornpone, ashcakes, and hoe cakes, made by Native Americans from their own recipes. It is also possible that other native foods such as pumpkin and squash were served." This is not to say that it was vegan or even vegetarian – there was deer meat as well as other flesh at the table – but the culinary focus of the harvest meal was plant foods. In fact, *Mourt's Relation: A Journal of the Pilgrims at Plymouth*, written by Edward Winslow and considered to be the best account of the harvest meal in 1621, does not explicitly mention turkey at the meal.

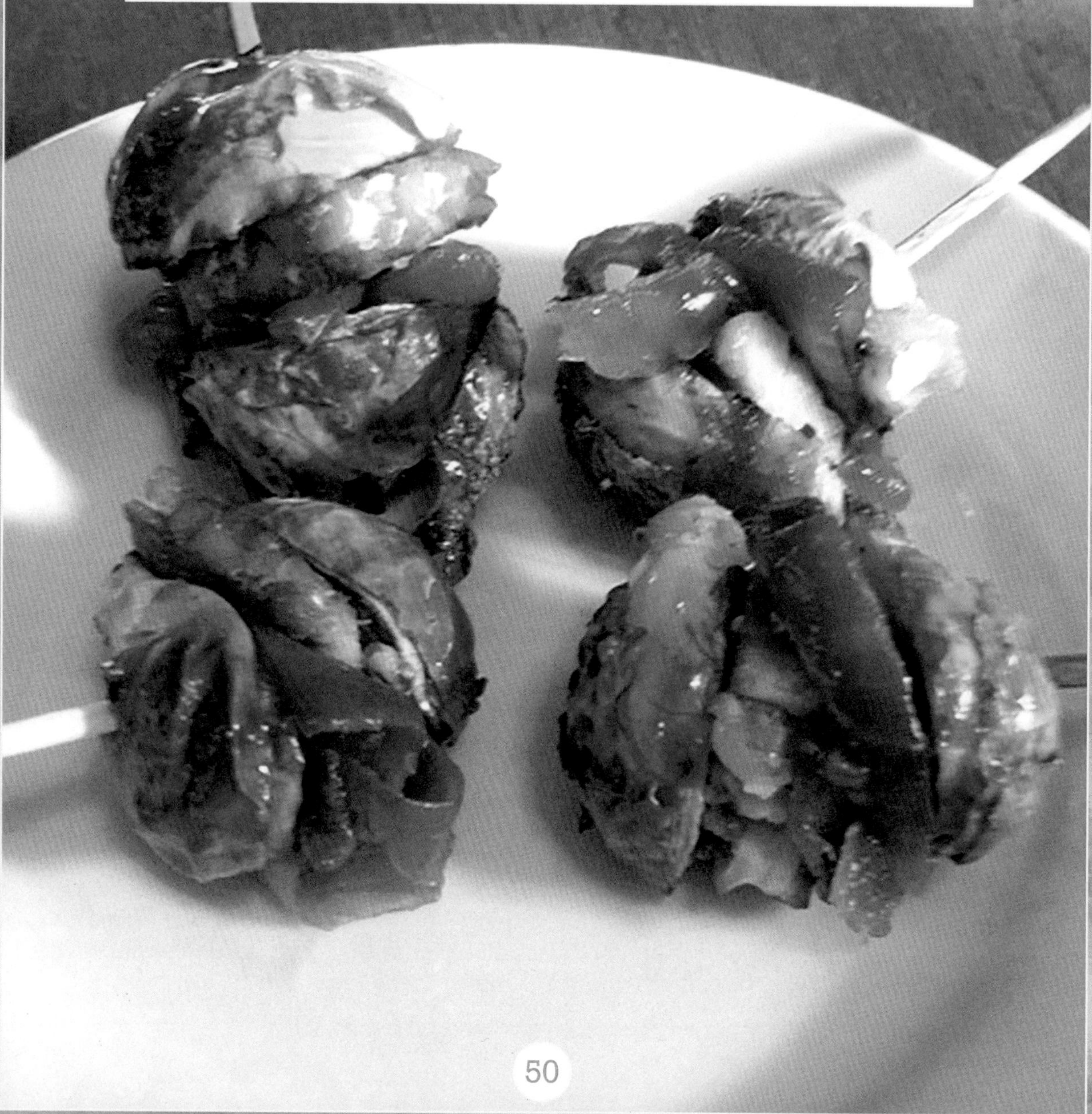

Appetizers and small bites
Brussels Sprout Sliders

I have a theory that 95% of people who don't like Brussels sprouts have never had them roasted, or roasted and stuffed with goodies and held together with toothpicks. (This is an untested theory.) Roasting Brussels sprouts helps them to manifest their glory as proud crucifers as opposed to the sad, boiled, gray mush we suffer through once a year at Thanksgiving. They become sweet, shot through with umami and tender to the bite. Paired with the equally luscious caramelized onions, a bit of assertive tang from mustard (always such a complement to Brussels sprouts, but you can use vegan mayo if you really are not a mustard fan) and some smoky tempeh, and you have an altogether new kind of slider, perfect as a unique appetizer for a holiday party, and a crazily addictive one at that. (If you are a tempeh hater, feel free to omit. I won't judge you. Okay, I will but it doesn't matter.) These are easy to make but a bit time and labor intensive; if you do make them, I think you'll agree that it was effort well spent. **Fun fact: This recipe was re-published in The New York Times!**

First, caramelize some onions.

2 large sweet or yellow onions, sliced thin
2 tablespoons olive oil
Salt to taste

Heat a large skillet over medium heat. Add the olive oil, heat for a minute, then add the onions and a sprinkling of salt. Stir frequently, making sure to stir from the bottom of the pan up, to dislodge any sticking onions. They will begin to yellow and shrink in volume, as they darken from yellow to more of a caramel color, lower the heat. Keep cooking until they are at the desired state. This usually takes between 25 - 35 minutes and they should be very brown – though not burnt – soft and sweet when you're finished cooking them..

Let cool.

Now, let's make the Brussels sprouts and tempeh.

Preheat the oven to 375 degrees.

20 large Brussels sprouts
2 tablespoons olive oil
1 tablespoon tamari
2 - 3 cloves garlic, pressed

Cut the Brussels sprouts in half from top to bottom and keep the two halves together. If you don't keep them together, you will have to search for a pair that fits well together after they've roasted, and screw that. Mix together the marinade in a bowl, and brush each Brussels sprout in the marinade. Remove and let sit cut side down on a parchment lined baking sheet. Let bake for 12 minutes, then turn the sprout, brush with any leftover marinade and bake seven more minutes.

8 ounces tempeh, cut into thin slices, side to side rather than top to bottom
2 tablespoons olive oil
1 tablespoons tamari
a dash of liquid smoke (if desired)
2 cloves garlic, pressed
1/2 teaspoon ground cumin
1/4 teaspoon cayenne pepper

Mix together the marinade in a rectangular baking pan and let the tempeh sit in it for 20 minutes, then turn all the pieces, pushing them in the marinade, and let them marinate another 10 minutes. Bake for 12 minutes, gently turn, and bake for 5 minutes more. If they seem dry, brush with some more tamari.

Cool onions, Brussels sprouts and tempeh for assembly.

Approximately 5 teaspoons grainy or Dijon mustard

Assembly:

Take one half of a Brussels sprout, smear the inside with mustard, add a piece of tempeh cut to fit the size of the sprout, add some onions (I used a melon baller for this), and take the other half of the Brussels sprout. Position it so the two sprouts are like the buns on a burger, with the cut sides facing each other. Secure with a toothpick: voila!

Warm on a baking pan in a 325 degree oven for 10 - 15 minutes.

Sweet Potato Bisque
with Crunchy Chickpeas

I love the contrast between the silky-smooth sweet potatoes and the crunchy but still chewy chickpeas. Allowing sweet potatoes to play with a great natural complement of ginger adds a nice little bit of spice and contrasting flavor. The small bit of peanut butter helps to create a creamy, dreamy bisque reminiscent of the classic West African groundnut stew but with all of those seasonal flavors we love, plus some unexpected additions that work together well.

1 large yellow onion, diced
4 cloves garlic, minced
1 tablespoon ginger, peeled and minced (optional, but I love it)
2 tablespoons tamari, divided
3½ cups sweet potatoes, peeled and diced
4⅓ cups low-sodium vegetable broth, divided
1¼ cups frozen corn, defrosted
½ cup vegan, unflavored creamer
½ lemon
2 tablespoons peanut butter
4 tablespoons Italian parsley, minced

In a medium soup pot over medium heat, warm 1/3 cup (or 1 – 2 tablespoons olive or coconut oil) for a minute. Add the diced onion, and sauté until softened, about five minutes, stirring often. Add the garlic, ginger and tamari, and sauté another 3 – 4 minutes. (Add more broth if needed.) Add the sweet potatoes, remaining tablespoon of tamari and four remaining cups of broth to the pan, raising the heat to medium-high. When it starts to boil, lower heat to medium-low, cover, and let simmer for 25 minutes, until the sweet potatoes are fork tender. Add the corn, creamer and peanut butter and cook five minutes more. Purée until creamy with an immersion blender or another blender; return to heat, season with salt and pepper to taste.

Turn off, squeeze the juice from ½ lemon in the pot and distribute to four bowls. Top with Italian parsley and Crunchy Chickpeas.

Crunchy Chickpeas

15 oz. cooked chickpeas, rinsed and drained
2 teaspoons olive oil
1 teaspoon ground sage
½ teaspoon dried marjoram
½ teaspoon dried rosemary
½ teaspoon dried thyme
1 teaspoon pepper

Preheat the oven to 400 degrees and link a baking sheet with parchment paper or a Silpat.

Mix the chickpeas and spices together in a bowl. Bake for 15 minutes, stir with a spatula, and bake for 10 more minutes.

★ Cornbread Muffins

It's a long list of ingredients these muffins are very simple to make and very worth it. Personally, I am partial to the Yankee-style cornbread that isn't very sweet, as opposed to the Southern style, which is sweeter. I like a cornbread muffin you can eat with the rest of your meal without it tasting like dessert. If you prefer a sweet cornbread muffin, remove some milk and add more maple syrup to replace that or you can also add sugar in the dry ingredients bowl. Coconut, maple or brown sugar would be a great choice.

2 tablespoons ground flax seeds
6 tablespoons aquafaba
or water (see page 107)
1 cup non-dairy milk
1 tablespoon apple cider vinegar
1¼ cups gluten-free flour (I used Bob's Red Mill 1-to-1 Baking Flour)
1 cup finely ground cornmeal
2 teaspoons baking powder
1 teaspoon baking soda

½ teaspoon salt
¼ teaspoon xanthan gum
⅓ cup sweet potato purée
¼ cup pure maple syrup
¼ cup refined coconut oil, other neutral oil, or melted vegan butter
1 cup frozen corn kernels, plus more for top

Preheat the oven to 350 degrees. Line a muffin tin with 12 liners.

Mix together the ground flaxseed and aquafaba in a cup. Place in the refrigerator. Mix together the milk and apple cider vinegar and place in the refrigerator, too. Allow to sit for ten minutes.

In a large mixing bowl, combine the flour, cornmeal, baking powder, baking soda, salt and xanthan gum. In a medium bowl, combine the milk mixture, flax mixture, sweet potato purée, maple syrup and oil. Pour into the dry ingredients and mix until about two-thirds combined. Add the corn kernels and mix until everything is incorporated.

Fill each liner about two-thirds full, top with a few corn kernels and bake for 17 minutes. Turn the pan, and bake 13 more minutes or until a toothpick inserted in the center comes out clean.

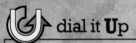 dial it **U**p

Serve warm with pats of vegan butter or jam.

Why did the fruit get interrogated by the police?

It was a persimmon of interest.

Didja Know?
The cornucopia derives from the Latin *cornu copiae* "horn of plenty." It is considered a symbol of abundance, which is why it has its place among holiday imagery but is much older than our Thanksgiving tradition, dating back to the 5th century.

Mains
The Whole Shebang
Vegan Thanksgiving Roast

Even since I first heard of the monstrosity known as turducken (do your psyche a favor and don't Google that if you don't already know), I've wanted to create a vegan version that played with the concept but, you know, not gross and horrifying. Tasty vegan noms, stuffed in tasty vegan noms, stuffed in tasty vegan noms, though, was perfect for my fickle attention span. Why not wrap a whole vegan Thanksgiving meal in flaky puff pastry? That will show them!

If you don't want to go the whole nine yards with making your own puff pastry, there is frozen vegan puff pastry dough on the market but it's not gluten-free and it's got hydrogenated oils in it; if you Google, you should be able to find it. The thing about this is that it's not hard, per se, but it does take hours of chilling time for your dough. If you go the DIY route, be sure to completely read through the instructions so you will know how much time is expected. (You'll need to start it the day before you need it.) It will also take some elbow grease, especially at first, to roll this out nice and flat but it is very doable. I recommend finding a surface for rolling that you can lean a bit on, in other words, one that isn't too high. Other than that, and the need to use vegan butter in the place of dairy butter, the Bob's Red Mill recipe and instructions worked like a charm without any issues. If you're not gluten-free, feel free to search for other vegan puff pastry recipes online and you will find a bunch. What I did here for everything else was just sort of follow the recipes that I wanted for the filling; feel free to substitute as you wish but I included the links to the recipes I used or were close to what I made.

The Whole Shebang Vegan Thanksgiving Roast (cont.)

Note: The ingredients listed below are all links to different recipes. Make each according to its instructions. Then we'll combine them all into one massive dish.

Note: this recipes uses ingredients made from several recipes. See the full list at **veganstreet.com/ thewholeshebang.html**

1 recipe gluten-free puff pastry, using the same amount of vegan butter
Mashed potatoes
Garlicky-lemony kale
Seared tofu cut in cubes or other shapes
Stuffing
Gravy
¼ cup aquafaba (see page 107)

Prepare the puff pastry as described and prepare your other recipes. Be aware that you will likely have excess of the filling and that is okay. Have everything cool so you can handle it. The last hour or two of the final chilling of your puff pastry is a good time to get everything else ready. Make sure your kale isn't too wet or it will make your puff pastry soggy. If you need to reheat your mashed potatoes a bit to keep them soft enough to spread, do that now.

Preheat your oven to 400 degrees and line a baking sheet with parchment paper or a Silpat.

Roll your puff pastry out into a long rectangle at about ¼ -inch even thickness over parchment paper or a Silpat. We cut off a bit to create a better rectangle and have some extra dough for decorating.

Spread a layer of mashed potatoes over the pastry, allowing an inch around the border without any so it doesn't smoosh out when you roll it.

Over the mashed potatoes, layer some kale.

Over the kale, layer your tofu and then the stuffing. This is all so delicious the instinct is to want to pack it all in but don't over stuff this or it will be very difficult to roll. Save the leftovers for something else.

To roll it, we folded up one long side in the Silpat (though it would work just as well in parchment paper) first and met it in the middle with the other side so it is shaped like a long log. If you have an extra set of hands available, it can be helpful. If there are tears or gaps in the pastry, it's okay. It's a very forgiving dough. Smooth it over. Close the ends.

Take the log and move it over to your prepared baking sheet. Brush with aquafaba, cut some slits for air vents in the dough, and decorate with any extra rolled bits of dough. Cookie cutter shapes also would work great. If you do adhere some extra pieces, brush over it again with your aquafaba.

Bake for 30 minutes, brush again with aquafaba, and bake for another 20 minutes. Allow to cool for about ten minutes, cut and serve with warm gravy.

Savory Holiday Pie

Coming out of the oven, this baby is impressive, no less impressive than **The Whole Shebang** *recipe on page 58. Our guests even gasped and took out their cell phones. Though it is quite a lot of steps and dirtied dishes, the Savory Holiday Pie is very easy to make and entirely worthwhile. Bring this to your holiday potluck and all the anti-vegans will be eating their words along with some tasty savory pie. Warm and filling, it is reminiscent of a shepherd's pie but with all the delicious flavors we associate with this time of year: Stuffing, greens, a hearty protein, mashed potatoes. Also, feel free to adapt the recipe as you like. For example, you can make it soy-free by using seitan or chickpeas for the tofu; use roasted Brussels sprouts instead of the kale; substitute barley for the stuffing. It's up to you.*

Note: this recipes uses ingredients made from several recipes. See the full list at **veganstreet.com/savoryholidaypie.html**

Vegan crust of your preference. You don't want to make a sweet crust because it's a savory pie. I used Breads from Anna Pie Crust Mix.
Stuffing
Mashed potatoes of your preference
Garlicky-lemon kale
Seared tofu
Gravy

Begin with your pie crust. Make according to instructions. I made my pie in a deep-dish pan. If you don't have that, two regular pie tins would work. Also, it doesn't need to be shaped like a pie. A casserole pan would also

Savory Holiday Pie (cont.)

work. Keep in mind that this will make too much stuffing and tofu for one recipe and you will have leftovers. Oh, no!

Meanwhile, start your stuffing as that will take the most time.

While the stuffing is cooking, start your mashed potatoes.

As those are cooking, make your kale and seared tofu. Preheat the oven to 375 degrees.

When the pie crust and the rest of the components are ready, start assembling. I put them in the order of tofu first (on the pie crust), then kale, stuffing and mashed potatoes. Shape the pie as you like. Sprinkle with chives, paprika, salt and pepper.

Bake for 25 minutes. Allow to cool for five minutes and serve. This is great with gravy on the side.

Desserts
Thanksgiving Day Chocolate Bark

Is chocolate really a traditional part of Thanksgiving? Not really. Do I care? Nope.

I made a version of this chocolate bark for last year's Thanksgiving celebration and it was devoured by a pack of hungry vegans in moments. Chocolate bark is shockingly easy to make, decadent and makes a great canvas for so many different add-ins you can tailor to what you are seeking. For this bark, I wanted to contribute familiar flavors of the season: cranberries (as in cranberry sauce), pecans and marshmallows (as in sweet potato casserole). The chewy tartness of the dried cranberries is a great complement to the crunchy, naturally sweet pecans; marshmallows are fun any time of year and the chocolate pulls it all together lusciously. Give it a try this Thanksgiving.

1 cup toasted, pecan halves, reserving 2 tablespoons for topping
¼ teaspoon salt
1 lb. vegan, slavery-free chocolate chips, reserving 2 oz. (see page 43)
1 tablespoons coconut oil
2 teaspoon pure vanilla extract
²/₃ cup dried cranberries
1 cup vegan mini-marshmallows (like <u>Dandies</u>) **or 1 cup regular vegan marshmallows, cut in half**

Preheat oven to 325 degrees. Place the pecan halves on a pie plate with a light sprinkling of salt and let bake for 6 - 8 minutes. Remove and you're done with the oven now.

Place parchment paper on a cookie sheet.

Heat a couple of inches of water into a simmer in a pot on the oven.

In a larger bowl, place the chocolate chips (reserving approximately two oz.) and coconut oil, stirring with a rubber spatula or wooden spoon until melted. Remove the bowl from the simmering pot, add the remaining chocolate chips, and stir to combine. Put the bowl back onto the pot and stir together until entirely melted, and then remove. Keep the water at a simmer, and be very careful to not get any water or steam into the chocolate or it can "seize."

Add all the dried cranberries and the toasted pecan halves, except for the remaining two tablespoons. Stir together until mixed well. Pour onto the prepared cookie sheet, spreading until flat.

On the top, intersperse the marshmallows and remaining pecan halves until pretty. Refrigerate until solid and enjoy!

Didja Know?

Buy Nothing Day is an international protest against the consumerism of Black Friday and 24-hour moratorium on shopping, held on either day after Thanksgiving or the Saturday after depending on locale. Promoted originally by *Adbusters* magazine, Buy Nothing Day was first organized in Canada in 1992 and has grown to include people from 60 countries across the globe.

Easy Pumpkin Cheesecake Cookies

Simple to make and richly decadent, these cookies are a great alternative to predictable Thanksgiving desserts. They take a while to cool but they are so worth it and make a great presentation.

16-ounces vegan cream cheese, softened at room temperature for 15 – 20 minutes
½ cup pumpkin puree
1½ cups all-purpose, gluten-free flour
½ cup coconut sugar or brown sugar
2 teaspoons baking powder
1 teaspoon pure vanilla extract

½ teaspoon ground cinnamon
¼ teaspoon ground ginger
¼ teaspoon ground nutmeg
⅛ teaspoon ground cloves
¼ teaspoon xanthan gum
Dash of salt
1¼ cups whole pecans
12-ounces slavery-free chocolate chips (see page 43)
1 tablespoon refined coconut oil

Preheat oven to 250 degrees. Spread pecans on a baking sheet and bake for five minutes, shake pan, then bake for 3 more minutes. Grind to a meal by pulsing in your food processor.

In a large bowl, combine the cream cheese, pumpkin, flour, sugar, baking powder, vanilla, cinnamon, ginger, nutmeg, cloves, xanthan gum, salt and ground pecans. You can do this by hand or in a stand mixer, using the paddle attachment. Cover the bowl and chill for an hour in the refrigerator.

Ten minutes before the hour is up, start tempering your chocolate as described on page 35. While the chocolate is melting, prepare two baking sheets with a piece of parchment paper on each.

Preheat oven to 350 degrees.

Scoop cream cheese mixture by ¼ cup or so and form into a slightly bigger-than- golf-ball shape with hands, than slightly flatten with hands. Place on two parchment-lined baking sheets. Bake for 13 minutes, turn 180 degrees, and bake another 8 - 10 minutes. Let cool for five minutes then transfer onto cooling racks.

Cool for 25 minutes.

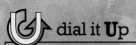 dial it **U**p

After dipping in chocolate, press in some crystallized ginger pieces on a plate.

Didja Know?

Fake foods? Turtle Island Foods debuted its first Tofurky Holiday Roast in 1995 but wheat gluten, a major component of the roast, has been around since the 6th century, first documented in China as a meat replacement for flesh-abstaining Buddhists.

Give a gift
to the entire world.
Go vegan.

VeganStreet.com
patreon.com/veganstreet

Christmas

I was raised Jewish but I went and married a blond goy from Minnesota so maybe there's a part of me that's a little bit of a shiksa? No, not really. That doesn't mean that I have anything against Christmas, though. I love the homey warmth of the season, the singing around the piano, the glad tidings and the visions of sugar plums dancing all around. Or maybe it's just like that in my imagination. No matter what you celebrate, if anything, you can always enjoy great vegan food and a chance to appreciate the blessings of the year.

Well, of course, I quit using reindeer after I went vegan, and then after a few months of green smoothies I felt so good I decided I could just pull this baby myself.

VeganStreet.com

Why was the child afraid of Santa?

He had Claustrophobia.

Lazy Christmas Morning Mint Hot Chocolate

This is what we have on Christmas morning. The mixture of cocoa powder and chocolate chips was born of not quite having enough of the cocoa left over after all the holiday baking but this unplanned improvisation results in a richer hot chocolate. Feel free to make up the difference in cocoa powder if you don't have chocolate chips or you want a drink without refined sweeteners. To me, nothing quite tastes like December than peppermint, so this is my favorite hot chocolate.

2 cups unsweetened plain almond or other non-dairy milk
2 tablespoons unsweetened cocoa powder
2 tablespoons maple syrup
2 tablespoons slavery-free vegan chocolate chips (see page 43)
½ teaspoon pure peppermint extract

In a medium saucepan, combine the milk, cocoa powder, maple syrup and chocolate chips, whisking over medium heat until everything is melted and combined. Keep warming until steam begins to rise but before it boils. Once you see steam, remove from heat, stir in the peppermint extract and enjoy.

Why did the walnut like the nutcracker?

It helped it come out of its shell.

Gingerbread Shake

"Gingerbread in a glass," is what our son calls this. With all of the flavors and aromas of gingerbread, this is a festive and fun drink, perfectly delicious any day or the year but especially fitting for the holiday season. Easy to whip up at a moment's notice with just a blender, this is easy to modify to your personal tastes. If you like more of a ginger kick, simply add more. Don't like cloves? Don't use 'em. Using a frozen banana is your best bet for a frothy, creamy shake, and the ice helps to make it even more of a frosty treat. Happy holidays!

1 frozen banana, sliced
1 cup plain, non-dairy milk
1 tablespoon pure maple syrup
1 teaspoon unsulphured molasses
½ teaspoon pure vanilla extract
¼ teaspoon dried ginger
¼ teaspoon cinnamon
¼ teaspoon ground nutmeg
⅛ teaspoon ground cloves
About 4 ice cubes

Combine together in a blender and blend until smooth. Pour and sprinkle with cinnamon for a little fun touch.

Cashew Coconut Eggnot

What would a pagan-leaning, agnostic Jewess like me know about a seasonal drink that is so quintessentially goy? Not much, truth be told. I have a vague recollection of helping my roommate make a conventional eggnog when I was a vegetarian and thinking that both the process and the taste was so beyond disgusting that for a long time, I had no desire to try it again. This is a drink that often calls for six or more eggs and the traditional preparation is for them to be served raw, though there are now cooked versions because who wants salmonella for Christmas? No one!

This is just the right amount of sweet for me and complemented with warming spices, rich cashew cream, creamer and plain almond milk. If you like it sweeter, just add more dates. The result is a creamy, custard-y and rich drink that is perfect for sipping around the piano while belting out your favorite vegan feminist numbers. It also lends itself beautifully to boozy add-ins but is quite complete in its virgin form. Enjoy over ice or just as is.

1 cup raw cashews or raw cashew pieces, soaked for four hours or overnight
½ cup water
2 cups plain vegan creamer (I used Trader Joe's coconut milk version)
2 cups unsweetened non-dairy milk (I used almond milk)

3 cinnamon sticks
1 teaspoon freshly grated nutmeg
½ teaspoon whole cloves
2 teaspoons pure vanilla extract
5 large medjool dates, pitted

* optional boozy addition: rum, whiskey, bourbon, etc.

Drain the soaked cashews and place in a blender (ideally high-speed but it will work with other blenders, it might just take a little longer) with a half cup of water. Blend until smooth. Meanwhile, in a medium saucepan, heat up the creamer, non-dairy milk, cinnamon, nutmeg and cloves. Bring to a boil, then lower to a simmer with a top on the saucepan for 15 minutes. Pour into the blender with the cashew cream, removing the cloves and cinnamon sticks. (I placed a small mesh colander on top of the blender to do this.) Add the vanilla and dates; blend until completely smooth. If it's too thick for your taste, add a little more milk. Transfer to a container and allow to cool for four hours or overnight. Before serving, give it a good shake. Serve with or without ice and an optional grating of whole nutmeg or cinnamon over the top.

Didja Know?
Many scholars believe that Christmas, which started being celebrated as the birth of Christ in the 3rd century, takes place on December 25 in order to coincide with the pagan Roman winter solstice festival of Saturnalia. The conversion of Emperor Constantine to Christianity in the 3rd century started the gradual process of transitioning Saturnalia into Christmas.

SAVORY CEREAL MIX

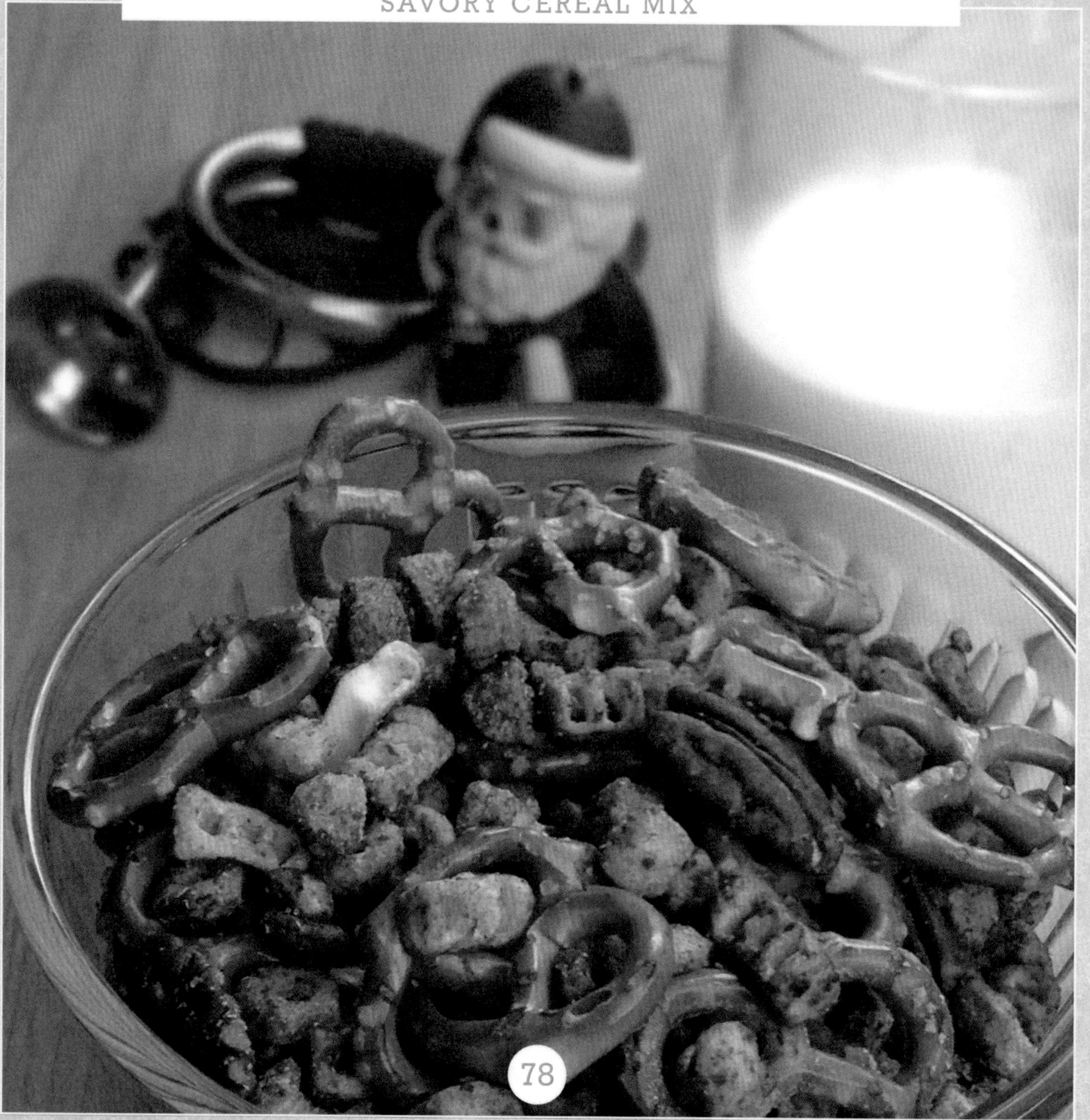

Savory Cereal Mix

Bowls of salty, crunchy things? Sure, sign me up. This takes a while to prepare because it cooks long and at a low temperature, but it couldn't be easier to make. I suggest keeping two timers going, one set at 1½ hours and one that you re-set every fifteen minutes. Feel free to use your favorite cereals in this.

9 cups assorted cereals (I used an "o" cereal, puffed millet, and a Rice Chex-type cereal)
1 cup nuts (I used pecans)
6 tablespoons melted vegan butter
¼ cup vegan Worcestershire sauce
2 tablespoons nutritional yeast
2 teaspoons granulated garlic
2 teaspoons granulated onion
1 teaspoon paprika
1 teaspoon salt
2 cups gluten-free pretzels

Preheat oven to 225 degrees. Get one or two long baking dishes. In a large bowl, combine your cereals and nuts. In a small bowl, stir together your butter, Worcestershire sauce and spices. Pour over and mix through your cereals. Pour bowl contents into your baking dish or dishes so the cereals are flat. Bake for 1 hour and 15 minutes, turning every fifteen minutes with a spatula. Add the pretzels, baking 15 more minutes, bringing the total baking time to 1½ hours. Season additionally as you like, cool, and serve.

Holiday Cheddar Ball

I grew up in the 1970s when the cheese ball reigned supreme so maybe I got some cheese ball fever by osmosis. I think I may have tasted it once or twice in my life but I very much remember the rich flavor and the feeling of fanciness. (You can take the child out of the 1970s but you can't take the 1970s out of the child.) Perfect for a holiday party, this vegan cheese ball has the same gently sweet, creamy richness - brought to us by the trustworthy cashew and easy, quick caramelized onions - as well as the zesty, savory flavor of the classic recipe. Don't be alarmed by the long list of ingredients: it makes a lot and it's very easy to make. Once the onions are done, it's all prepared in one bowl.

2 teaspoons olive oil
1 tablespoon low-sodium tamari
1 cup yellow onion, diced
Extra water or low-sodium vegetable stock, as needed
2 cups raw cashews, soaked for an hour and drained
1 cup roasted red bell pepper
8-ounces vegan cream cheese
⅓ cup refined coconut oil, liquid
2 teaspoons vegan Worcestershire sauce (Whole Foods Market has a gluten-free store brand if you are looking for one)

1 tablespoon miso paste (try a dark miso for a sharper taste,
a light miso for a mellower flavor)

⅓ cup nutritional yeast

2 teaspoons onion powder

1 teaspoon garlic powder

½ teaspoon mustard powder

½ teaspoon smoked paprika

1 teaspoon salt

⅛ teaspoon cayenne powder

2 capsules vegan probiotic powder (acidophilus)

1 cup toasted, lightly salted walnut pieces

Heat a small or medium pan over medium heat for a minute. Add the olive oil and spread it around, heating for 30 seconds to a minute. Add the onions and tamari, stir together, and lower the heat to medium low. Keep sautéing, stirring often, for 15 - 20 minutes, adding more water or stock as needed to keep the onions from sticking and burning. You definitely don't want it to burn! They should be a deep golden brown and soft throughout.

Combine the cashews and roasted red bell pepper in a food processor and mix together for a minute. Add the rest of the ingredients, including the caramelized onions, and remove the probiotic powder from their capsules, adding just the powder.

Process for three to four minutes, pausing to scrape down when necessary, until smooth. Place contents in a bowl and refrigerate for 4 - 6 hours or overnight. When firm, spread your toasted walnut pieces in a single layer in a pan, and shape your chilled cheese into a ball. It'll be sticky but it's okay. Roll around in the walnuts so it's all coated and place on your serving plate or platter. Ideally, chill again and serve cold with crackers.

Mains

Sweet Potato, Black Bean and Corn Tamales

A beloved tradition to those of Mexican heritage, making tamales means Christmas. It is conjectured that the filling in the middle of the tamale symbolizes the baby and birth of Christ. Tamales are delicious and very thrifty to make but can be intimidating: there are a lot of steps. While that is true, it is also pretty easy and there is no need to let the steps stand between you and some tasty tamales. As always with a recipe, read through the directions first so you know what to expect and to have on hand. The trick here is to have your assembly stations prepped because it makes everything so much easier. The assembly is what makes it smart to double or triple this recipe and freeze the prepared tamales, which is why the tamalada – tamale prep party – tradition exists. Load up on supplies, grab some friends and you'll be rich in tamales for the near future.

15 – 16 cornhusks (hoja de tamal)**, soaked for an hour to soften**
1 teaspoon olive oil
1 yellow onion, diced
1 cup cooked black beans, rinsed and drained
1 cup frozen corn, defrosted
2 teaspoons ground cumin
Salt and pepper to taste
½ tablespoon fresh lime juice
2 cups masa harina
2 teaspoons baking powder

Sweet Potato, Black Bean and Corn Tamales
(cont.)

½ teaspoon salt
2 cups low-sodium vegetable broth, warmed
¼ cup olive oil
¼ cup sweet potato puree

Warm olive oil in a medium pan over medium heat for a minute. Add onions and sauté over medium-high heat for about 6 – 7 minutes, stirring often, until onions get softened and begin to get golden. Add the black beans, corn, cumin, salt and pepper, sautéing until the corn is cooked through, about three minutes. Turn off the heat and squeeze on and mix through the lime juice.

On two large, flat pans like cookie sheets, spread out nine cornhusks with the tapered end toward you. Fill a medium pot with enough water that the bottom ¼ is covered. Bring to a boil and then a simmer. Have your steamer basket near your assembly station. This needs to be deep enough that the tamales can be stood up in it with a lid on the pot. In a large bowl, mix together the masa, baking powder, salt, warm vegetable broth, olive oil and sweet potato puree until thick and smooth. Spread about ⅓ cup of masa on the cornhusk, into a 3-inch square, about ¼-inch thick. (Doesn't need to be exact.) Leave about ½-inch free of masa on the sides.

Place a tablespoon or two of the black bean filling in the middle of the masa. Pick up the two long sides of the cornhusk and bring them together folding them to one side and rolling around the filling. Fold up the empty part of the tapering end to form a closed bottom and tie with a "rope" pulled off your extra cornhusks. It might be easier to pie two of these ropes together. Tie this around the bottom of your tamale to hold the flap in place; fold over the top and secure this with another tie. Place this upright in your steamer basket. Do each tamale the same way, filling up your steamer basket. If there is room left in the basket, fill this with any extra cornhusks to keep the tamales from moving too much.

Lower the heat on the pot on the over to simmer. Place the steamer basket with tamales on it and cover. Steam for one hour.

Serve warm with salsa, guacamole and anything extra you might like.

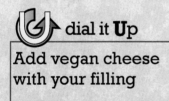 dial it **U**p

Add vegan cheese with your filling

Which tubers are the kindest?

Sweet potatoes.

Didja Know?
One explanation for the tradition of hanging stockings for Christmas stems from the story that upon hearing about a poor merchant who couldn't afford gifts for his three daughters, St. Nicholas tossed three bags of gold coins down the chimney of the merchant's home, knowing that he wouldn't accept charity if he'd been given it directly. The bags of gold fell into the girls' stockings, which had been hung by the fireplace mantle to dry. As the story spread of St. Nicolas' largesse, hanging stockings on Christmas Eve became a tradition.

Desserts
Oatmeal Chocolate Chip Cookies

With the old trick of applesauce and a couple other cards up my sleeves, these Oatmeal-Chocolate Chip Cookies are modified from a favorite old recipe, and they are crunchy on the outside and chewy on the inside, with hits of melted chocolate in every bite. In other words, they taste like the oatmeal cookies you might have loved in the past, but they are gluten- and oil-free. These are also refined sugar-free, save for the chocolate chips. If you want to be truly virtuous, substitute raisins for the chocolate chips but a friend of mine once said, "I think raisins in cookies are mean," and I have to admit, I kind of agree. (Please note that while oats are naturally gluten-free, unless they are processed on dedicated equipment, there is a risk of cross-contamination with gluten-containing grains, thus those with Celiac disease would need to make this with designated gluten-free oats.)

Makes about 22 cookies

Preheat oven to 325 degrees F. Line a cookie sheet with parchment paper or lightly brush with oil.

¾ cup rolled oats

Process in a food processor or a blender until pulverized to a coarse flour.

½ cup pure maple syrup
¼ cup "no sugar added" applesauce
2 tablespoons non-dairy milk (I usually use unsweetened almond)
2 teaspoons vanilla extract

In a small bowl, whisk together the above until integrated.

¾ cup rolled oats
1 cup gluten-free flour (I use Bob's Red Mill 1-to-1 Baking Flour)
1 cup vegan, slavery-free chocolate chips (see page 43)
2 teaspoons baking powder
½ teaspoon baking soda
½ teaspoon salt
½ teaspoon allspice

In a separate, larger bowl, add the above and the ground oats. Pour the wet ingredients into the dry and mix until it is well incorporated.

Scoop out heaping tablespoons of batter onto the prepared cookie sheets. You can roll them between your hands for a neater cooker or leave them alone for a more rustic look.

Bake for 11 minutes, then rotate the cookie sheet 180 degrees and bake for 6 more minutes.

Cool and enjoy!

Chocolate Crinkle Cookies

These cookies feature my favorite baking trick: puréed sweet potatoes. Sound like something you'd only can imagine being fed a Gerber baby? Well, I can see that, but when you bake with it, puréed sweet potatoes offer a silky, voluptuous texture to gluten-free sweets (so often dry, crumbly and heavy), and it also heightens the sweetness without adding refined sugar or overwhelming flavor. The most important thing to me when I am baking my gluten-free and oil-free vegan treats is that they are still treats. I don't want to feel like I'm doing anything too virtuous but I still don't want to break the bank in terms of empty calories. Using the purée and the old trick of applesauce, I can have my cookies and eat 'em, too. Of course, chocolate chips never hurt, either. (I never said I was a perfect angel.)

They are easy to make, turning into cookies that are a little crispy on the outside, domes of billowy chocolatey goodness on the inside. Please factor in refrigeration time when making these babies.

1½ cups gluten-free flour (I used Bob's Red Mill 1-for-1 Baking Flour)
⅓ cup unsweetened, slavery-free baking cocoa (see page 43)
2 tablespoons arrowroot flour

1½ teaspoon baking powder
1 teaspoon ground cinnamon
½ teaspoon salt
⅔ cup pure maple syrup
½ cup puréed sweet potato
½ cup unsweetened applesauce
2 teaspoon pure vanilla extract
1 cup slavery-free vegan chocolate chips (see page 43)
Confectioners' sugar, optional

In a large bowl, whisk together the flour, cocoa powder, arrowroot, baking powder, cinnamon and salt. Combine the maple syrup, puréed sweet potato, applesauce, and vanilla in a small bowl with a whisk. Pour into the larger bowl with the flour, and mix with a spoon until integrated. Add the chocolate chips and fully incorporate.

Transfer to the 'fridge and let it sit there, covered, for at least an hour. This makes it easier to shape the dough into balls and will reduce the spread on the baking sheet.

Preheat oven to 350 degrees. Using about one tablespoon per cookie, roll into balls with your hands and place on a parchment-lined cookie sheet. To create a pretty little snow-dusted effect, roll each cookie on a plate with some confectioners' sugar before placing on the baking sheet. Bake for eight minutes, turn 180 degrees to ensure even baking, and bake for another eight minutes. Remove from the oven and let sit on the cookie sheet for five minutes and then let cool on a wire rack.

Christmas Day Chocolate Bark

Did you know that you can make beautiful and expensive-looking chocolate bark in the comfort of your own home? I have been making this recipe for years and I am always impressed by the creative opportunities that chocolate bark lends itself to: you can make a Thanksgiving version (as you see in this book), a Valentine's Day version and even a summer version. You are just limited by your imagination. For this one that is embracing the Christmas season, I've chosen just a few flavoring elements because I just didn't want to get between chocolate and mint. Those two are pretty tight. This makes an elegant, simple bark that makes a great holiday present, contribution to the office potluck, addition to a Christmas stocking (just remember to wrap it!) and on and on. With a minimum of effort, you will get a great little treat. Enjoy!

16 oz. slavery-free, vegan chocolate chips (see page 43)
½ tablespoon coconut oil
1 teaspoon pure vanilla extract
½ teaspoon peppermint extract
²/₃ cup broken peppermint candy canes or candies, broken*
(I used and recommend TruJoy candy canes, made without artificial dyes and with organic sweeteners)
Salt for sprinkling on top

Line a cookie sheet with parchment paper.

In a double-boiler or a DIY double-boiler (how I roll) with a few inches of simmering water in it, add your chocolate chips and oil, reserving two tablespoons of chocolate chips. (The oil is necessary to get it to melt uniformly; you can also use vegan shortening.) Stir until all is melted, turn off the heat and remove the bowl, add the reserved chocolate chips and stir until they are melted. Add the vanilla and peppermint extracts and stir some more.

Spread the chocolate across the sheet evenly. Sprinkle the broken candy canes across the top, then sprinkle with a bit of salt. Store in the fridge until it sets. Cut or break into individual pieces and serve.

* I just broke my pieces with a knife on a flat board but I would imagine pulsing in a food processor would work just as well. Use a very light touch, though, because you don't want these to be pulverized into powder.

Didja Know?
The Guinness Book of World Records records that the world's largest snowflake was reported to be 15-inches across and 8-inches thick and was documented at Fort Keogh, Montana on January 28, 1887.

Soft Peanut Butter Ginger Spice Cookies

One of my favorite combinations is peanut butter and ginger. I was introduced to this when I was in my 20s and a local restaurant called Logan Beach Café had Indonesian night once a month or so. This was where I first discovered how beautifully peanut butter pairs with ginger and it was this first taste experience that inspired these cookies. Spiced with cardamom, cloves and other warming spices, these cookies are not your standard peanut butter cookies and the crystallized ginger takes it to a whole different realm. These gently sweet cookies are moist on the inside with crunchy exteriors and full of complex, aromatic flavor notes. These are peanut butter cookies for grown up tastes.

1 tablespoon ground flax
3 tablespoons aquafaba or regular water (see page 107)

Dry ingredients
1¼ cups gluten-free all-purpose flour
1 teaspoon baking powder
½ teaspoon baking soda
1 teaspoon ground cinnamon
½ teaspoon cardamom

½ teaspoon ground ginger
¼ teaspoon ground cloves
⅛ teaspoon salt

Wet ingredients
¾ cup smooth peanut butter
1 tablespoon real vanilla extract
½ tablespoon blackstrap molasses
3 tablespoons unsweetened applesauce OR neutral oil
½ **cup real maple syrup** (if you like a sweeter cookie, maybe also add some coconut sugar or brown sugar)
½ **cup crystallized ginger, chopped small, reserving 2 tablespoons**

Preheat the oven to 350 degrees and line two cookie sheets with parchment paper.

In a cup, stir together the flax and aquafaba or water with a fork or a mini-whisk. Store in the fridge for 15 minutes.

In a large bowl, whisk together your dry ingredients. In a medium bowl, stir together the wet ingredients and add the flax goop. Add to the dry and stir; add the crystallized ginger, reserving two tablespoons. It will be thick.

Roll a tablespoon or two of batter between your hands and place on your prepared cookie sheets. Flatten with a fork to make the classic peanut butter cookie back-of-the-fork marks to make a crisscross or just flatten with your hands. Sprinkle the tops with the reserved crystallized ginger, bake for 12 minutes, and allow to cool on the sheets for 10 minutes.

Candy Cane Brownies

These Candy Cane Brownies were invented as a way to scratch that itch for sweets without going overboard. Exchanging maple syrup and brown rice syrup for sugar helps to boost the nutritional profile a bit (or maybe make it just not quite as indulgent) and switching in sweet potato puree for oil makes this treat a lot less calorie-laden but still full of rich flavor. These brownies aren't exactly health food – eat fruit for that – but they are close enough while still tasting like a treat and with the peppermint candy canes, perfectly flavored for the season. These come out rich, dense and minty, perfect for the winter holidays.

1 tablespoon ground flax seed
3 tablespoons aquafaba
(see page 107)
½ cup pure maple syrup
¼ cup brown rice syrup
1¼ cups gluten-free all-purpose flour
½ cup slavery-free cocoa powder
(see page 43)
2 teaspoons baking soda

⅛ teaspoon salt
¾ cup sweet potato purée
1 tablespoon pure vanilla extract
¼ teaspoon peppermint extract
½ cup, plus two tablespoons slavery-free, vegan chocolate chips, divided (see page 43)
1 - 2 full size, vegan candy canes (not mini or giant ones), **crushed***

Preheat the oven to 325 degrees. Line a 8-X-8 baking pan with parchment paper or lightly grease.

In a cup, mix together the flax and aquafaba with a small whisk or fork. Allow to sit for 15 minutes in the fridge.

In a small saucepan, heat together the maple syrup and brown rice syrup over low heat until integrated and more liquid-y.

In a medium bowl, combine all your dry ingredients – the flour, cocoa powder, baking soda and salt. In another bowl, mix together the syrups, extract, flax mix and sweet potato purée. Pour the wet into the dry ingredients; fold in ½ cup of the chocolate chips. (If the syrup is still warm, this will melt the chocolate chips, which is fine.) Mix together until you have a smooth, thick batter. Spoon into your prepared pan and top with reserved chocolate chips.

Bake for 20 minutes. Turn 180 degrees and bake for five minutes. Sprinkle the crushed candy canes and bake 10 more minutes. Allow to cool.

* A handy way to crush candy canes is to put them in a plastic bag and roll over them with a rolling pin or hit with a hammer.

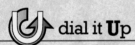 dial it **Up**

Keep all the ingredients the same except add ¼ cup neutral baking oil and use ¼ cup less sweet potato purée. (I recommend melted refined coconut oil.)

Didja Know?
Horror film staple Boris Karloff, perhaps best known as the monster in James Whale's 1931 *Frankenstein*, won a well-deserved Grammy Award in 1967 for his voiceover work as the title character and narrator on the recorded version of *How the Grinch Stole Christmas*.

New Year's Day

I may be an oldster but for me, the fun of the new year is all about the day after New Year's Eve. New Year's Day, there is no pressure to stay up late and have The Best Night Ever, less danger on the road, and it's a relaxed day of reflection and hope for the year ahead. Okay, yeah, I just read that: I am *definitely* an oldster. Be that as it may, my family has a tradition of having friends over for a New Year's Day brunch potluck and it's sooooo much fun! (In an oldster kind of way.) We hang out, enjoy one another's company, share our hopes and plans for the year ahead - as well as burn pieces of paper upon which we've written what we'd like to leave behind - and enjoy fabulous food together. It's certainly better than waking up in a tacky motel in Vegas in a pile of barf with a new wedding band on and a stranger beside you. (What would I know about that?)

Which New Year's Day food has the worst reputation for being pugnacious?

Black-eyed peas.

New Year's Revolution

VEGAN

Let's Make This the Year.

VeganStreet.com

Cranberry Apple Sparkling Drink
with Cranberry Ice Cubes

Overdoing it on the sugary foods this season? It's hard to avoid with all the temptation around us from Thanksgiving until we start being little angels again on January 1. A lot of the commercial sparkling juices are delicious but very high in sugar. This is a low-sugar drink you can enjoy with a great seasonal appeal and not a lot of calories. Plus, polyphenols, the antioxidant compound found in cranberries, has been shown to help improve circulation and kidney function. Kids and adults alike can enjoy it; if it's too sour for a young palate, just add a bit more apple juice. The cranberry ice cubes are completely unnecessary but a little festive touch.

Cranberry Apple Sparkling Drink
¼ cup cranberry juice (no apple juice added, just pure cranberry juice)
¾ cup sparkling mineral water

Mix the apple and cranberry juice in a 16-ounce glass. Add ice and fill to the top with mineral water.

Cranberry Ice Cubes
about 32 cranberries
Water

Fill your ice cube tray half-way with water and freeze. Add the cranberries, two in each compartment, and fill the rest of the way with water. Freeze.

Lucky New Year's Day Greens

Leafy greens are a classic part of a New Year's Day menu because many believe they are a symbol of money and prosperity in the year ahead. Collards are the traditional greens but any hearty leafy greens would work; kale would make the most obvious replacement here. This dish - succulent and full of bright, nourishing flavor - is my version of the classic creamed greens recipe but it's lighter and more robust. If you're not a nutritional yeast fan, feel free to leave that out but I like the subtly cheesy taste it lends to the dish.

⅓ cup low-sodium vegetable broth
1 yellow onion, diced
3 cloves garlic, minced
2 bunches of collards, stems removed and cut into 1-inch wide strips
1¼ cups low-sodium vegetable broth
½ cup raw cashews (can be pieces or whole), soaked for an hour unless using high-speed blender
2 tablespoons nutritional yeast (optional)
1 tablespoon low-sodium tamari
1 tablespoon fresh lemon juice
Crushed red pepper, salt and pepper to taste

Heat the ⅓ cup vegetable broth in a large skillet over medium-high heat for one minute. Add the onion and sauté for five minutes, until beginning to be softened. Add the garlic and sauté three minutes, stirring often so it does burn. Add more broth by the tablespoon if needed.

In a blender, combine the broth, cashews, optional nutritional yeast and tamari. Blend until smooth.

Add the collards to the skillet and mix together for a minute. Add the blender contents and sauté for five minutes or until softened. Turn off the heat, add the lemon juice, optional crushed red pepper, salt and pepper. Serve warm.

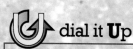 dial it **U**p

Use olive oil or refined coconut oil instead of vegetable stock for the sauté.

Glam it up

Serve in a casserole pan with some toasted panko, breadcrumbs or ground nuts to the top (almonds would be nice) to serve as an au gratin-style recipe.

Didja Know?

Between 40% - 50% of people in North America will make a New Year's resolution and most of those resolutions fall under the category of self-improvement. According to research, more than 20% of these resolutions fail after one week and almost all are abandoned after twenty-four months. According to research published in *Forbes*, the resolutions with the greatest likelihood of sticking are simple - think small, attainable goals rather than one giant achievement - specific and measurable (as opposed to vague) and are publicly stated to make yourself more accountable.

Hoppin' John Burgers

I usually eat some form of black-eyed peas on January 1, a customary food in the U.S. believed to help usher in prosperity to those who eat them on the first day of the new year. I don't know if they will bring prosperity but I still love black-eyed peas: they cook quickly for a legume (no soaking required), and they are full of fiber. One year, I decided to turn these into burgers. The result was a burger that was soft and flavorful on the inside, crispy on the outside, thanks to the sesame seeds (actually, some cultures consider sesame seeds good luck, too). They take a little time but they are easy to make and truly delicious. Serve hot from the oven or warm up in a skillet coated with a little oil. Load up with your favorite fixings - especially lucky greens! - and dig in.

2 cups dried black-eyed peas, sorted

1 cup quinoa

1 yellow onion, diced

¼ cup low sodium vegetable broth

3 garlic cloves, minced

1 teaspoon dried thyme

1 teaspoon dried basil

½ teaspoon smoked paprika

¼ teaspoon red pepper flakes

1½ cups crushed tomatoes

1 tablespoon gluten-free tamari

½ cup garbanzo bean flour

4 scallions, sliced thin

2 tablespoons fresh chives, minced

Salt and pepper to taste

1 cup sesame seeds

Cook the black-eyed peas in plenty of water, at least 12 cups. Partially cover and bring to a low boil over medium-high heat. Cook for an hour or until the black-eyed peas are soft. Drain.

While the black-eyed peas are cooking, combine the quinoa with two cups of water in a small pot and bring to a boil, then simmer, covered, over medium-low heat until the water is absorbed and the quinoa is tender, about 15 minutes.

In a large skillet, heat the vegetable stock over medium-high heat for a minute, then add the onions. Cook for 4 - 5 minutes, until the onion is beginning to soften, then add the garlic, spices, crushed tomatoes, tamari and salt and pepper. Simmer for 20 minutes over medium heat, occasionally stirring.

Preheat oven to 350 degrees. Cover a baking sheet with parchment paper or lightly brush with oil. Spread the sesame seeds on a large plate.

Place half of the cooked black-eyed peas in a food processor and purée until smooth. In a large bowl, combined the puréed black-eyed peas, remaining beans, quinoa, tomato-onion mixture, garbanzo bean flour, scallions, chives and any additional seasoning. Mix together with a large spoon. The mixture should be thick. Scoop up 1/3 cup, roll into a ball, then roll each one in the sesame seeds, coating it completely. Place on the prepared baking sheet, press to lightly flatten, and continue until the sheet is full.

Bake for 20 minutes, gently flip, then bake for 17 more minutes. Serve warm with all your fixings. Enjoy the new year!

Cheesy Tater Tot & Cauli Casserole

Sometimes we all need a little comfort food and when my family does, this dish one fits the bill, tasting like something that might have come from a zany vegan family, circa 1956. I mean that in the best possible way, of course.

This dish came together out of laziness, frankly, and me not wanting to go to the grocery store. Looking around, I had frozen tater tots (don't judge me!), a cauliflower that was beginning to feel rejected and the components of a cheesy sauce. After that initial trial, this has become one of our favorite go-to winter dishes, something my son's friends always love as well. Feel free to raise the nutritional profile by subbing diced sweet potatoes for the tater tots, adding spinach, and so on. The idea is creating a baked casserole of vegetables and a cheesy sauce. With tasty veggies smothered in a warm, savory sauce that evokes melted cheese (hey, though, it manages to be fat-free), Cheesy Tater Tot and Cauli Casserole manages to be nourishing and nurturing at once.

1 head cauliflower, broken into florets
½ yellow onion, diced
¼ cup low sodium vegetable stock
2 tablespoons tamari or soy sauce, divided
½ tablespoon olive oil
1 ½ lbs. frozen tater tots

Cheesy sauce
½ cup garbanzo bean flour
2 cups low-sodium vegetable broth
2 cups plain, unsweetened vegan milk (I used almond)
½ cup nutritional yeast

Cheesy Tater Tot and Cauli Casserole (cont.)

2 teaspoons dried basil
1½ teaspoons granulated garlic
1 teaspoon dried thyme
1 teaspoon dried dill
Salt and pepper to taste
1½ cups frozen peas, defrosted
2 tablespoons sherry vinegar
or fresh lemon juice
Paprika

Preheat your oven to 400 degrees.
Line a baking sheet with parchment paper or lightly brush with oil. Mix together with cauliflower, onion, stock, 1 tablespoon of tamari and olive oil in a large bowl, then spread on the baking sheet. Bake for 18 minutes, then turn with a spatula, add remaining tablespoon of tamari, and bake for 8 more minutes.

Meanwhile, also bake the tater tots according to the package instructions. (Mine also baked at 400 degrees, so I cooked them at the same time as the cauliflower.) Leave your oven on.

Meanwhile, make your cheesy sauce.

Whisk together the flour, broth and vegan milk in a medium saucepan until mixed together. My technique is to add the liquid to the flour a little bit at a time to control lumps better. Don't worry about lumps too much, though, because you will dissolve them when you cook this sauce.

Heat to medium-high and add the nutritional yeast and spices, whisking often until the sauce begins to slow boil and thicken, about 8 minutes. Lower the temperature if it starts bubbling too high, you want a slow boil. When it's thick, add the peas, stirring until heated through. Remove from heat and add the vinegar or lemon juice.

In a long rectangular pan, line up the tater tots in an adorable fashion at the bottom of the pan, then add the prepared cauliflower on top of that. Gently pour and spread the cheesy sauce on top of the cauliflower and sprinkle with paprika, making sure to cover all the cauliflower. Cover with aluminum foil and bake for 25 minutes in your 400 degree oven.

Let it sit for five minutes with the foil on, then remove, serve and enjoy!

All About Amazing Aquafaba

I wrote about the discovery of aquafaba at **veganstreet.com/veganmeringuecookies.html** and ever since its discovery, it has taken the world by storm with its easy replacement of egg whites. With the discovery of aquafaba, all these foods and drinks that were once off the table for vegans and those with egg allergies are back on it again. How cool is that?

Aquafaba is the liquid leftover from beans, either canned or from cooked dried beans and three tablespoons of aquafaba will usually replace one egg. I tend to use only chickpea water for my aquafaba because I like its mild flavor but others have found success with other varieties. Their FAQ page answers most questions and there is a very active Facebook page I encourage you to join to see all that is possible with this humble ingredient. Visit **aquafaba.com** to learn more

Magic Peanut Butter Pretzel Bars

Okay, this took me a few times to get just right. The union of peanut butter (savory), pretzels (salty) and chocolate (sweet) is a match made in heaven but it took some trial runs in the kitchen before I got the complementary textures down. The first time the peanut butter was too heavy. I tinkered with the peanut butter and got it right. Then the chocolate was too runny and, over-correcting it the next time, the chocolate was too hard and tasted fine but broke into less than pretty bits when slicing and serving. Now, with a sweet-crunchy date-nut crust, a creamy, mousse-like peanut butter filling, and a smooth, dense ganache topping, I think we have the perfect union. There are a lot of ingredients here but, trust me, it's super easy to make.

Crust

1½ cups soft medjool dates, pitted
2 cups pecan pieces, toasted
½ cup gluten-free pretzels
1 tablespoon real maple syrup

Lightly oil or place parchment in a 9-X-13-inch pan.

If your dates are tough, soak them in hot water for 30 minutes, then drain.

Place your toasted pecan pieces and pretzels in a food processor and pulse until crumbly. Add the drained dates and maple syrup. Pulse until combined. Press into the prepared pan.

Peanut Butter Mousse

1½ cups creamy, natural peanut butter
8-ounces firm silken tofu, drained
½ cup plus two tablespoons pure maple syrup
1 teaspoon real vanilla extract
⅛ teaspoon salt

Combine all the ingredients in your food processor and process until smooth. Spoon on top of the crust, flattening with the back of the spoon or a silicone spatula and refrigerate for 30 minutes.

Chocolate Ganache Topping

2 cups plain, nondairy milk
12 ounces slavery-free, vegan chocolate chips (see page 107)
1 teaspoon real vanilla
1 cup gluten-free pretzels, broken into small bits

Heat your vegan milk to hot on the stove top. Place the chocolate chips in a medium bowl you can cover with a lid or plate. When the milk is at a low boil, pour to cover the chocolate chips – you might have to shake the bowl to cover everything – and place the lid over the bowl. Allow to sit for five minutes then whisk from the center out until smooth, adding the vanilla extract. Pour over the peanut butter mousse and sprinkle the remaining pretzel bits over the top.

Refrigerate for 30 minutes to an hour and serve.

This Valentine's Day, share your heart with all beings.

VeganStreet.com

Valentine's Day

Ugh, so much pressure! Whether you are single or in a relationship, Valentine's Day is all about celebrating romantic love. What about the other kids of love? Plato and Aristotle wrote of *philia*, or friendship, love; *storge*, or familial, love; *agape*, or universal, love; *ludus*, or playful, love; *pragma*, or pragmatic, love; *philautia*, or love for oneself. Wouldn't the world be a better place if we simply loved more? No matter what kind or kinds of love you are celebrating this Valentine's Day, the most important thing is to have an expansive, generous heart.

Why was the compost bin such a popular Valentine?

It was always full of a-peel.

Love for All...
Great & Small
We are working for the day & when all creatures know freedom & joy

photo: Barry Bland
VeganStreet.com

CHERRY PIE SHAKE

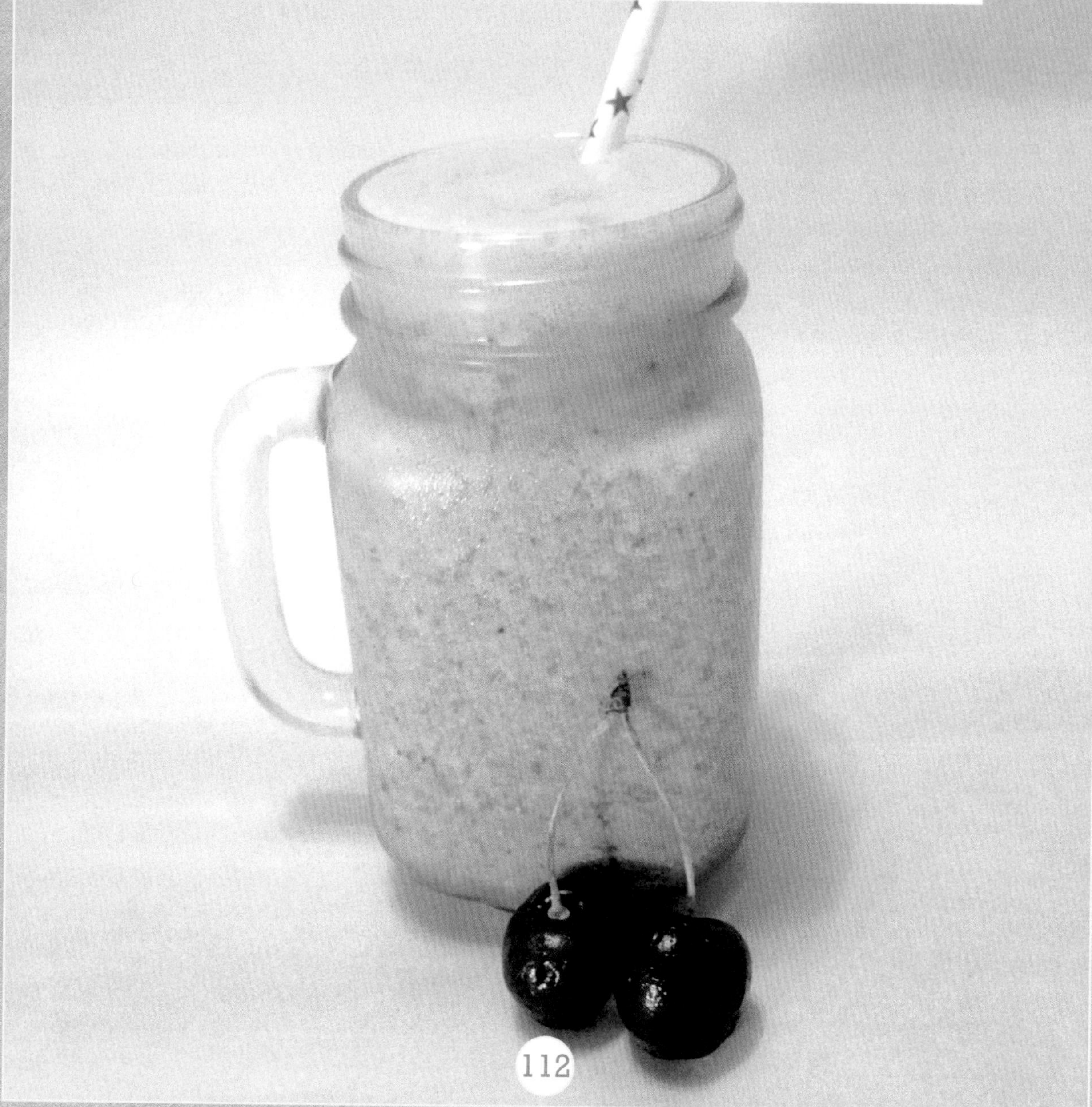

Drinks
Cherry Pie Shake

This refreshing shake is easy to make and takes delicious advantage of that blessed little stonefruit, cherries. What more could you want?

4 cups plain non-dairy milk
1 tablespoon pure vanilla extract
¼ cup real maple syrup
⅓ cup soaked cashews, drained
2 bananas
1 cup frozen or fresh cherries, stemmed and stones removed
1 cup ice

Add all ingredients to the blender and blend.

Didja Know?
The origin of the phrase "to wear year heart on your sleeve" also dates back to the Middle Ages, when unmarried people would pick a name out of a bowl to see who their love might be and would wear the name pinned onto their sleeves for one week.

Which melon is least likely to get married?
Cantaloupe

Herbed Gluten-Free Focaccia Bread

One of the hardest things about being gluten-free is the absence of bread, delicious bread. There isn't much that is more alluring to a longtime wheat-avoider than bread - warm, comforting, filling bread. Recently, I got a craving for focaccia bread and it just wouldn't quit. I developed this recipe to sooth that craving and I have to say, I couldn't be more pleased: not only did it turn out just how I wanted it to – soft, savory, rich and buttery – but now I think I've got sandwich bread, pizza dough and more implanted in the DNA of this combination of ingredients. Ah, sweet bread! This recipe takes a bit of time with the risings but it is easy to make and entirely worth it, making two loaves. Keep in mind that the mix-in herbs and extras I chose are totally suggestions and can be modified to your preferences. Please note that you will need a stand mixer for this recipe.

½ **cup unsweetened, nondairy milk** (I used almond)
½ **cup aquafaba** (see page 107)
½ **cup water**
2 **tablespoons olive oil**
1 **packet active yeast**
1 **tablespoon pure maple syrup**

2¼ cups all-purpose, gluten-free flour (I used Bob's Red Mill)
1 teaspoon baking powder
1 teaspoons salt
1½ teaspoons xanthan gum

Additional mix-in options: I used ½ cup vegan Parmesan, ⅓ cup sun-dried tomatoes (tender but not oil-packed ones), 3 tablespoons sliced kalamata olives, 2 tablespoons fresh rosemary, 1 teaspoon red pepper flakes. Other options might be fresh basil or oregano, roasted bell pepper or nutritional yeast.

Gently heat the milk, aquafaba and water until lukewarm in a small pot. Whisk the olive oil and yeast into the pot and allow to sit until the surface is bubbly. Add the maple syrup and whisk again.

In the large bowl of a mixer, combine the flour, baking powder, salt and xanthan gum. Add the yeast-milk mixture to the flour and stir until smooth. Allow it to sit, covered, for 30 minutes.

After 30 minutes, mix on high in a stand mixer with the paddle attachment for three minutes. When done, stir in your mix-in options and cover; allow to sit 30 more minutes. Be aware that your batter will be more like cake batter than bread batter. This is to be expected at this stage with gluten-free baking.

Divide into two lightly oiled (bottoms AND sides) 8- or 9-inch round pans and smooth the top with a silicon scraper. Preheat the oven to 375 degrees and allow the dough to rise another 15 minutes.

Bake for 20 minutes.

Immediately turn out on a cooling rack. If it sticks, run a knife along the edges and knock on the bottom of the pan. Best, avoid this by oiling your pans.

Roasted Cauliflower Curry Soup

Luscious, fragrant and flavorful, this is perfect for Valentine's Day.

1 cauliflower, cut into florets (about five cups)

1½ cups Yukon potatoes, skinned and diced

1 yellow onion, diced

2 carrots, cut into ½-inch coins

3 - 4 cloves garlic, minced or pressed

1 - 2 tablespoons fresh ginger, minced

1 tablespoon neutral oil (I used melted refined coconut oil)

1 tablespoon tamari

4 cups low-sodium vegetable stock

14 oz. lite coconut milk

1 tablespoon curry powder

1 teaspoon ground cumin

½ cup raw cashews, soaked for one hour and drained*

½ tablespoon fresh lemon juice

Salt and pepper to taste

Minced herbs or toasted cashews (optional)

Preheat the oven to 400 degrees.

Fit a piece of parchment paper to a baking sheet or shallow roasting pan. In a large bowl, combine your veggies up to the ginger. Mix with the oil and tamari, stirring until all veggies are covered. Spread flat on your baking sheet and cook for 18 minutes, then mix around with a spatula and cook for 15 more minutes.

Meanwhile, blend the vegetable stock, coconut milk, curry powder, cumin and cashews together until smooth. Pour into a large pot along with the roasted veggies and cook over medium heat for seven minutes. Using an immersion blender or blending in batches, blend the soup until smooth. Turn off the heat and add the lemon juice. Taste for additional salt or pepper. Ladle into bowls and sprinkle with minced herbs or toasted cashews.

* If you have a high-speed blender, you don't have a need to soak your cashews.

Didja Know?

Lovebirds in the US are believed to have begun exchanging hand-made valentines in the early 18th century but it wasn't until the 1840s when Massachusetts-born artist and entrepreneur Esther A. Howland began selling the first mass-produced valentines, made out of lace, ribbons, embossed flowers and colorful illustrations through her company, the New England Valentine Company. Long before Henry Ford, Ms. Howland developed an assembly-line approach to constructing her painstakingly handcrafted cards, employing women and helping them earn a living. At its height, her company earned $100,000 a year, making her quite a success in the 19th century. As a side note, the "Mother of the American Valentine" never married.

Mains
Sweet Potato Gnocchi with Sage-Butter Sauce for Lovers

So I learned a couple of things while developing this recipe:
1. Gnocchi are flipping adorable.
2. The reason they have those little ridges in them is for sauce to settle in. (Ingenious!)
3. They are much easier to make than they look.
4. Sooooo good!

Seriously, dumplings are found the world over and for food reason: they are the quintessential comfort food. Gnocchi, an Italian classic traditionally made very much like this recipe but with eggs, takes the humble dumpling and elevates it to an elegant stature. I got over the eggs with sweet potatoes, which add a richness, baking powder and the addition of aquafaba. Still, honestly, it's mainly just potatoes and flour. When you see your first gnocchi rise in the water, though, I doubt you'll be able to contain yourself.

Like most flour-related things that require shaping, there are some steps to this but it is easy and quick. This is a good recipe to develop your cooking intuition on, too, because you want the dough to be smooth, not too dry and not too sticky. For the sauce, I chose a simple butter sauce because I really wanted these babies to be center stage, not drowning under a heavy sauce. Feel free to improvise as you like. The sage adds a bright, earthy vibrancy as does the lemon at the end. Prepare for someone you love. (This includes you!)

Sweet Potato Gnocchi with Sage-Butter Sauce for Lovers (cont.)

1½ pounds potatoes (I used two sweet potatoes and one russet), **rinsed, skins on**

1¼ cups gluten-free, all-purpose flour (plus extra for dusting your surface and any more you might need)

3 tablespoons aquafaba (p 107)

1 teaspoon salt

½ teaspoon baking powder

Sage-Butter Sauce

4 tablespoons vegan butter

½ cup fresh sage, chopped or leaves whole

Salt and pepper to taste

Crushed red pepper flakes (optional)

1 tablespoon fresh lemon juice

Preheat your oven to 400 degrees. Prick the potatoes several times over with a fork. Bake the potatoes for one hour or until a fork can easily pierce them and remove skins when cool. Alternatively, steam the same amount of peeled and diced potatoes for 25 minutes or until fork tender. In a large bowl, mash the potatoes with a potato masher until combined and smooth. Add the flour by the half-cup until firm and no longer sticky.

On a floured surface, knead the dough for a couple of minutes, adding flour by the tablespoon if it sticks to the surface.

Start a large pot of salted water to boil.

Gather the dough into a mound and cut into four equal pieces. Ball each section in your hands and roll back and forth into a rope about 18-inches long, about the width of a thumb. (This doesn't need to be exact.) Cut each piece into an inch long piece, then press with the bottom of a fork or a gnocchi board. While pressing, shape the bottom around your finger so it is gently curved. Or don't. It's just an aesthetic thing.

In a large sauté pan, melt your butter over medium heat and add the sage. Once the butter melts, lower to medium-low.

Drop your gnocchi into the boiling water in batches. As they finish cooking, they will float, which will be after about two minutes. Using a slotted spoon, remove the gnocchi as they rise to the surface, drain them, then place in the sauté pan with the butter-sage sauce. Once all have been boiled and are in the pan, cook a little longer, adding salt, pepper and optional crushed red pepper flakes to taste. Turn off the heat, pour on the lemon juice, stir and serve warm.

Chocolate Raspberry Tart
with Crystallized Ginger

With tart, bright raspberries tempered with slightly spicy ginger and everything enrobed in a luscious, velvet-y chocolate ganache, this is a great way to treat your Valentine.

When we first made this recipe, the new camera could fall into the bowl of ganache. Plop. It happened in slow motion. It happened in an instant. It was the best of times. It was the worst of times. (No, it really wasn't the best of times by anyone's interpretation.) Chocolate driblets sloshed over the side of the bowl. I think they may have even been shaped like teardrops. I fired and broke up with my photographer/husband in one fell swoop. But as he sat frantically licking, q-tipping, and wiping off the camera, I remembered that this recipe is to celebrate Valentine's Day. I have my not-so-great moments, too. I vowed in sickness and in health - or the woo-woo equivalent with our acupuncturist-presiding-as-minister when we got married - and I meant it. There was no vow addressing the accidental dropping of cameras into warm ganache but it's implied, I think. When we found the right person, we forgive.

This tart makes forgiveness easy. With a cookie-like press-in crust, the aforementioned ganache and flavors that meld together beautifully, we realize that life is too short to hang on to petty grievances. He fixed the camera, by the way. (Apparently treating a camera like a mother cat would a baby kitten who has fallen into soot worked for us.) My husband is equal parts Clark Griswold and MacGyver and I love him for it. Make this for your favorite screw up this Valentine's Day and you won't regret it.

Chocolate Raspberry Tart with Crystallized Ginger (cont.)

1 cup quick oats
²⁄₃ cup raw pecan halves
3 tablespoons pure maple syrup
2 tablespoons melted coconut oil
½ teaspoon ground cinnamon
½ teaspoon ground nutmeg
¼ teaspoon salt
13.5 oz. full-fat coconut milk
(in a can, not a carton)
2 tablespoons pure maple syrup
2 teaspoons vanilla extract
12 oz. slavery-free, vegan chocolate chips (see page 43)
1 cup frozen or fresh raspberries (I used frozen)
2 tablespoons crystallized ginger, cut into smaller pieces

Lightly oil the bottom of a 9- or 10-inch springform pan.

Preheat the oven to 350 degrees. Place the pecans in a pie plate or square baking pan and bake for five minutes. Remove from oven and allow to cool for a few minutes.

Grind the oats in a food processor for two minutes, until finely ground. Add the pecans, cinnamon, nutmeg, maple syrup, coconut oil and salt. Let it process until it sticks together well. Press into the bottom of the springform pan and bake for 13 minutes. Remove from oven and allow to cool.

In a small pan, bring the coconut milk and maple syrup to a boil over medium-high heat. Remove from heat and stir in the vanilla.

Put the chocolate chips in a medium or large bowl. Pour the coconut milk mixture over the chocolate chips, stirring until thick and smooth.

Clean and dry the food processor and pulse the frozen raspberries, 4 - 5 times, until they are shaped like uneven pebbles. If using fresh raspberries, just coarsely chop. Stir into the bowl with the chocolate.

Add the crystallized ginger, taking care to drop the ginger pieces in separately as they tend to clump. (Don't drop the camera!) Stir until everything is incorporated and pour over the prepared crust.

P.S.: This would be pretty garnished with fresh raspberries but that is very out of season for us right now, so we went without. Instead, we held a paper doily over the tart and shook powdered sugar over it in a fine-mesh colander. This only took three sets of hands to accomplish.

Liberate
Your Seder Plate
by celebrating a cruelty-free Passover.

With some simple replacements, no animals need
to be harmed to celebrate your holiday.

Passover

Passover to my family when I was growing up was always spent at my grandparent's condo in the city. Not only was it a chance to hang out with my beloved grandparents, it was a time to spend with my extended family of aunts, uncles, cousins, and on and on. Though it was cramped, it was always a really great time. Today, we spend Passover with friends and we celebrate it without dead animals on the table. The Passover story is all about liberation and standing up for those who are oppressed, thus the vegan message and practice fits seamlessly with this holiday, bringing extra meaning and poignancy to the meal. Though a vegan seder isn't traditional, it is consistent with the emphasis on living a life of compassion that is emphasized within Judaism.

Didja Know?

On a vegan Passover seder plate, the traditional roasted shank bone is often replaced with a roasted beet and the hard-boiled egg might be replaced with a white eggplant or an orange.

How could the Pharaoh fail to notice all the Jews escaping Egypt?

He too deep in de-Nile.

Appetizers and Small Bites
Mock Chopped Liver

With Passover, I feel the need to add another question to our list from the Haggadah: Does anyone really like chopped liver? Okay, there are maybe three people in the world who like chopped liver, one of those is on the fence and none will even publicly admit it. It was the only thing my grandmother made that I would have to give the side-eye to, even as a kid who loved everything my grandmother cooked and didn't really think twice about eating anything put in front of me. Chopped liver, though, that was a different story.

That said, what's not to like about a mushroom-cashew-lentil pâté (unless you don't like mushrooms, in which case, eh, sorry)? (Hey, this is a great opportunity to share a joke from my son: why does the shitake get invited to all the parties? Because he's a fungi. Get it? He's a fungi. Don't forget to tip your server…) What my mock chopped liver misses in terms of ground organ unctuousness, it makes up for in sheer umami creaminess. Schmear on crackers or matzo and it can be enjoyed any time of the year.

1 cup green lentils
3 cups low-sodium vegetable broth
1 bay leaf
2 tablespoons olive oil, divided
1 large yellow onion, diced
3 cloves garlic, minced
1 tablespoon tamari
2 cups sliced bella baby mushrooms
1 cup toasted cashews
1 teaspoon onion powder
1 tablespoon lemon juice, or to taste
Salt and freshly ground pepper to taste

In a medium pot with a lid, cook the lentils, broth and bay leaf over medium heat. Cook for thirty minutes. The lentils will not absorb all the water but they should be soft. Remove the bay leaf.

Meanwhile, in a large skillet, heat 1 tablespoon of olive oil over medium-high heat. Sauté the onions for about five minutes, then add the garlic, mushrooms and tamari, sautéing until the liquid has evaporated, about 10 minutes, stirring occasionally.

In a food processor, pulse the cashews and cooked lentils until combined. Add the mushroom-onion mixture, lemon juice, onion powder, last 1 tablespoon of olive oil, salt and pepper and process until smooth. Add any broth or water by the tablespoon to make it more smooth. Chill and serve.

Quinoa Stuffed Bell Peppers
with Toasted Pine Nuts and Cashew Feta

Creating a main dish for herbivores during Passover is no small feat, especially with gluten and grains off the table. Thankfully, today we have quinoa, the tiny but mighty seed that behaves like a grain in recipes. A complete protein containing all nine essential amino acids, as well as being fiber-, iron- and magnesium-rich, the little seed packs a powerful nutritive punch and when combined with seasonings, can help to create a flavorful dish.

*For this recipe, I wanted to create a main dish that was substantive but also elegant and, most important, tastes amazing. Passover has quite the laundry list of food restrictions so I wanted to create something that tasted complete in and of itself, something that could be enjoyed any time of the year, and I think these stuffed peppers do the trick. With a flavorful quinoa pilaf packed into bell peppers topped off with cashew feta baked to crispy perfection on top, this dish makes a pretty presentation while remaining filling and delicious. If you don't like bell peppers or can't find them, feel free to stuff roasted portobellos, zucchini, winter squash or whatever floats your boat. Note that I include peas in this recipe as legumes were recently stricken from the prohibited foods for Passover by a group of rabbis who know better than I do about Jewish law (see the next **Didja Know**) but if you still stick to the legume ban, feel free to replace the peas with something else. A quick note: because the peppers will be baked standing up, choose ones with wide, flat bottoms.*

Quinoa Stuffed Bell Peppers
(cont.)

Cashew Feta

1 cup raw whole cashews or pieces, soaked until soft (about four hours) **and drained**
2 teaspoons fresh lemon juice
1 capsule vegan probiotic powder (acidophilus)
1 teaspoon granulated garlic
Salt to taste

Place the cashews, lemon juice, probiotic powder, granulated garlic and salt in a food processor and pulse until crumbly.

6 bell peppers (ideally red, yellow, orange or a combination)
Olive oil to brush the outside of the peppers
1½ cups quinoa, rinsed
3 cups low-sodium vegetable broth

1 cup frozen peas, defrosted
½ cup toasted pine nuts
1 tablespoon dried dill weed
1 teaspoon salt
½ teaspoon ground pepper

Move the rack in the middle of the oven if it isn't there now. Preheat the oven to 375 degrees. Lightly oil a rectangular baking dish or line with parchment.

In a medium pot, cook the quinoa in the vegetable broth until beginning to boil; lower the heat, cover, and simmer for 20 minutes. Fluff with a fork.

Didja Know?

The story of Passover tells us that when God lead the Jews out of bondage in Egypt, there was no time to allow bread to rise, which is why the holiday is commemorated by avoiding wheat, barley, rye, spelt or oats, at least in their leavened form, during the week of Passover. Legumes are also banned by many Ashkenazi Jews during Passover because, according to a 13th-century edict, they are often stored near grains and can be cross-contaminated with them. In December of 2015, though, 19 rabbis from the Conservative branch of Judaism came together to issue a repeal on the legume ban. While not all who observe the holiday have embraced the legume during Passover week, it suddenly got a lot easier for Jewish vegetarians who do.

Place the peas and the toasted pine nuts in a large bowl, cover with the cooked quinoa, and season to taste with dill, salt and pepper.

Cut the stems out of the tops of the peppers, leaving access to the large cavity for stuffing. Remove any membrane and seeds. Lightly brush the outside with oil and stand on their bottoms in the baking dish.

Stuff the peppers with the quinoa filling and top with the cashew feta, gently packing down, reserving six tablespoons for later. Cover the baking dish loosely with foil and bake for 25 minutes. Remove the foil, increase the temperature to 400 degrees, and bake 20 more minutes. When the peppers are softened and the tops have a slightly charred crust, remove from the oven, sprinkle with a tablespoon or so of reserved cashew feta and serve.

Glam it up

Add sun-dried tomatoes and/or olives to the quinoa pilaf.

VEGAN MERINGUE COOKIES

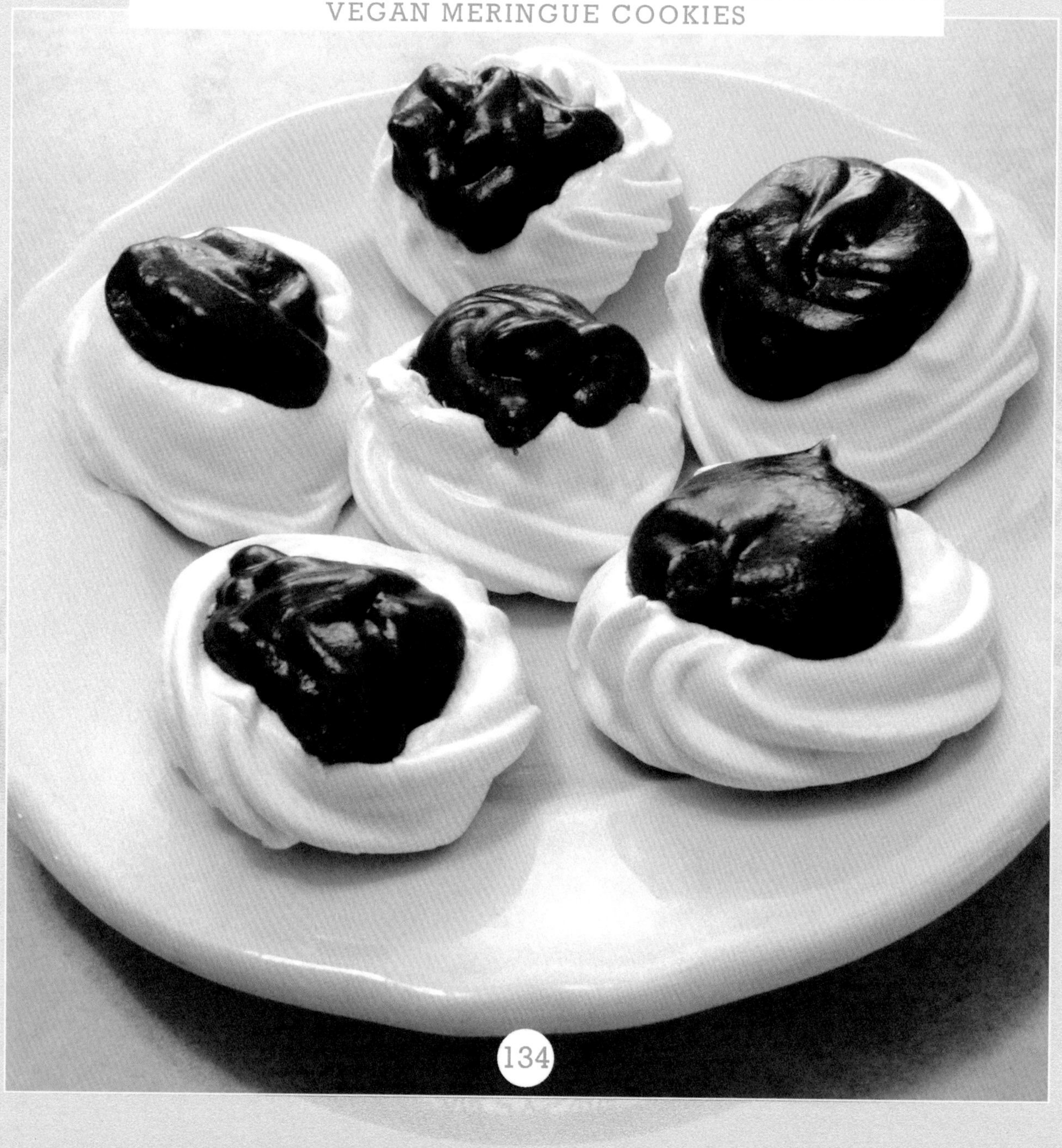

Vegan Meringue Cookies
with Chocolate-Almond Butter Ganache

What did we do before the discovery of aquafaba? I don't want to remember.

These meringue cookies can be enjoyed any time of the year but with spring here in our part of the world, we are celebrating new beginnings and excitement for the future so I think this is the perfect time. We can find reasons for hope with this new vegan meringue and its place at the Passover table, giving thanks that we can live in a world full of fantastic discoveries that can bring us closer to our compassionate ideals all the time.

Liquid from one 15.5 ounce can chickpeas (aquafaba) (see page 107)
½ cup organic sugar
1 teaspoon pure vanilla extract
¼ teaspoon cream of tartar

Ganache

12 ounces slavery-free, vegan chocolate chips (see page 43)
½ cup vegan milk, unsweetened
(I used almond)
1 tablespoon coconut oil
¼ cup almond, peanut or cashew butter

Vegan Meringue Cookies
(cont.)

Drain your chickpeas and reserve the beans for another use.

Whip the bean water and the cream of tartar on high until you begin to have ridges. Begin to add your vanilla and then your sugar by the tablespoon until it is all added. Some people have found success using a hand mixer but my understanding is that stand mixers consistently work the best.

Whip constantly for 15 minutes. Now you have vegan meringue!

Squeeze the meringue into table-size dollops onto a Silpat or parchment-lined baking sheet. I used a pastry syringe but you can also use a pastry bag or even a small plastic bag with the corner snipped off.

Bake at 200 degrees for 1½ hours, then remove from the oven and make a small indentation with your finger or a teaspoon. Place back in the oven for 30 more minutes.

Meanwhile, make your ganache.

Place your chocolate chips in a bowl with the coconut oil. Warm your milk to hot, then pour over the chocolate chips. Cover with a plate and let it sit undisturbed for a minute or two. Take the plate off, whisk, and combine, adding in the almond butter. Let this sit and thicken for about ten minutes.

Add to your pastry bag, a plastic bag or a small spoon and top your cookies as you like. They are ready to enjoy right away.

When does a vineyard feel best?

When it's grapeful.

Chocolate Raspberry Mousse

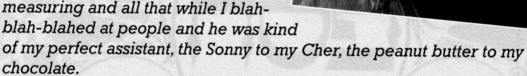

I had the really great opportunity to do a cooking demo at Veggie Fest, one of the biggest vegetarian festivals in the world. I am not afraid of public speaking but the idea of doing a cooking demo was a little intimidating; I still jumped at the chance. Thankfully, I was able to rope my husband into doing the measuring and all that while I blah-blah-blahed at people and he was kind of my perfect assistant, the Sonny to my Cher, the peanut butter to my chocolate.

I decided that I wanted to demo a dairy replacement and an egg replacement. For the dairy replacement, I wanted to make something really rich and luscious so I went with this Chocolate-Raspberry Mousse that I kept refining until I got to this final recipe. (Literally, in bed the night before the demo, I was making mental modifications.) This is very easy to make and super tasty; it's good as a mousse and it's thick enough to also be good in a crust and served like a French Silk pie. If you are avoiding soy, you can make this with 100% cashews, though it will be more dense and less creamy. If you don't eat legumes at Passover, swap the tofu for cashews, too.

6 ounces slavery-free vegan chocolate chips (see page 43)
4 tablespoons plain, unsweetened almond milk
(or dairy-free milk of choice)
12 ounces frozen raspberries, thawed
1 (12 ounce) package firm silken tofu
1 cup cashews, soaked in water for one hour or more and drained
(pieces or whole is fine)
1/3 cup real maple syrup
2 teaspoons pure vanilla extract
¼ cup slavery-free vegan cocoa powder (see page 43)
Pinch salt
Whole raspberries for garnish (optional)

Melt the chocolate chips and almond milk in a pan over medium-low heat until smooth.

Place in a fine-mesh sieve resting over a bowl. Using the back of a spoon, push the raspberries through the sieve, extracting as much juice from raspberries as possible. Save the remaining crushed raspberries for another use, like a smoothie.

Place drained cashews, silken tofu, maple syrup, raspberry juice, vanilla extract, cocoa and melted chocolate in a blender or food processor. Blend until smooth, about a minute.

Pour mixture into a bowl (or pie crusts) and place in refrigerator for at least two hours to allow mousse to firm up. When ready to serve, divide among bowls and top with fresh raspberries.

Easter

I don't have much of a personal history with Easter but I do love bunnies and brunch so that's all I need to know. One of our favorite traditions when my son was little was dyeing turnips with beets, turmeric, blueberries and onion skins and hiding them in our back yard. Yes, my son will probably be in therapy for life but there are worse things. Today, we skip the dyed turnips and head straight to brunch. Again, there are worse things.

What kind of rabbit makes the biggest mess?

A dust bunny.

My son with his basket
of dyed turnips –
Easter 2005

(yes, we really did that)

Things Are About to Get a Whole Lot Less Cute.

Each Easter season, thousands of people purchase baby rabbits for their children. More than 80% of these creatures are given up as soon as they get less "cute". A few lucky ones are rescued by animal shelters, but most let outside die from starvation or predators. Don't buy bunnies. If you adopt one, they usually live for 10-12 years.

Source: Huffington Post

VeganStreet.com

Appetizers and Small Bites

Cream of Broccoli Soup

This Cream of Broccoli Soup is the result of my interest in developing recipes that are filling without being high calorie and less seasoned without being bland. This soup is creamy and silky from the potatoes and has an element of cheesy goodness imparted through the nutritional yeast and miso. It has kind of a spring-y, light taste and is especially good with a squeeze of lemon and some generous pepper.

4 cups broccoli crowns, sliced
3 heaping cups Yukon potatoes, peeled and diced
1 yellow onion, diced
2 cloves garlic, minced
½ tablespoon low-sodium tamari
2⅓ cups low-sodium vegetable stock, divided
2 cups plain, unsweetened almond milk
¼ cup nutritional yeast
1 tablespoon light miso (I used chickpea)
Lemon and fresh ground pepper for serving (optional)

First, begin steaming your broccoli and potatoes. Set a pot with a few inches of water over medium-high heat and, once boiling, set a steamer basket with your broccoli and potatoes over the top, covered. Steam for 13 – 14 minutes or until the potatoes are soft enough to be easily pierced with a fork.

Meanwhile, in a medium sauté pan, heat ⅓ cup of vegetable stock over medium-high heat. Heat for a minute, then add the onions. Sauté for four – five minutes until softened, then add the garlic and tamari. Lower the heat to medium and cook, stirring often, for about 12 minutes or until browned.

Add your steamed potatoes and broccoli to a blender along with the onion mixture. Add the remaining two cups of stock as well as the almond milk, nutritional yeast and miso. Purée until smooth. Return to your cooking pot and cook until heated through.

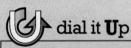 dial it **U**p

Add some soaked cashews to the blender when you purée the mixture, like ¼ - ⅓ cup. If you do, you may need to increase the broth.

Didja Know?
It is believed that the Easter tradition has its etymological roots in Eostre or Ostara, the Germanic goddess of spring and dawn. Eostre, referred to by Jakob Grimm in his Teutonic Mythology as the goddess of "the growing light of spring," and was associated with eggs and the rabbit, symbols of new life, and this has carried over to Easter iconography and celebrations today.

Herb-Mashed Potatoes

A variation of the famous Irish dish calconnon, these mashed potatoes have spinach but also bright, vibrant flavor from fresh dill and chives. It's also easy, quick and inexpensive to make.

12 Yukon gold potatoes (approximately 6 cups)**, peeled and diced**
½ cup plain non-dairy milk
2 tablespoons vegan butter or olive oil (optional but recommended)
2 cups baby spinach
2 teaspoons garlic granules
2 tablespoons minced dill
2 tablespoons minced chives
Salt and pepper to taste

Heat a large pot of water over medium-high heat. When it starts to boil, add the potatoes. Cook for 10 – 12 minutes or until tender.

Meanwhile, in a small pan, heat the milk and butter over a low flame until the butter melts.

Drain the potatoes and mash with the warm milk, spinach and garlic. Mash until smooth, adding milk by the tablespoon if it's too dry. Stir in the minced herbs and mix until incorporated. Salt and pepper to taste.

What did the lemon call the reamer?

It's main squeeze.

DILL-EDAMAME HUMMUS

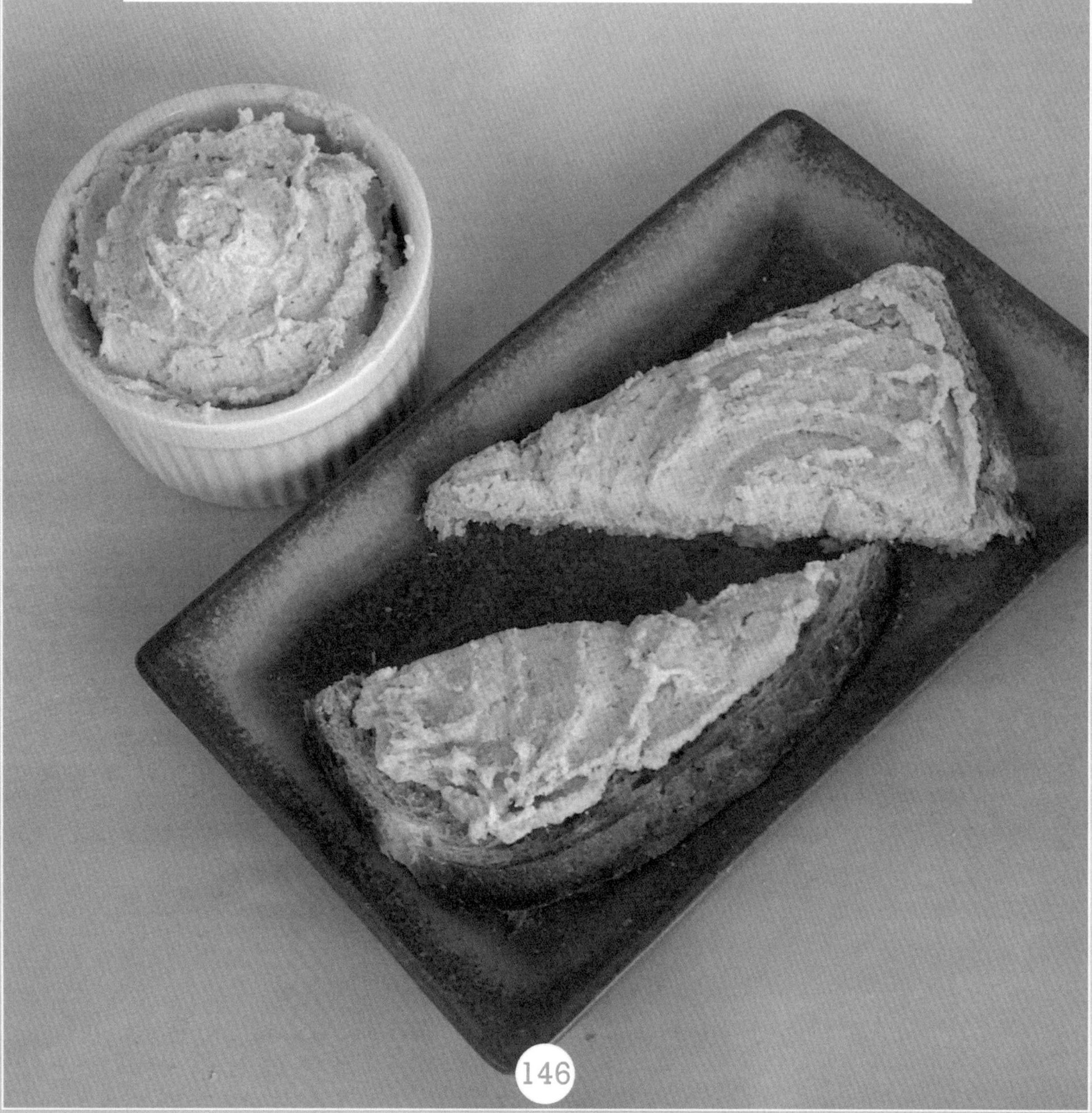

Dill-Edamame Hummus

Like many longtime herbivores, I have eaten my weight three or four times over in hummus by this point of my life but somehow it never gets old. Especially because you can easily make hummus from home and flavor it just as you like, the humble bean paste is surprisingly versatile. This version is great for springtime with its soft green color and lively dill flavor, but it is also rich, creamy and packed with protein.

15½ ounces cooked chickpeas (reserve water)
9 ounces cooked, shelled edamame (green soybeans)
¼ cup tahini plus one tablespoon
4 tablespoons aquafaba or regular water (or more) (see page 107)
1 tablespoon minced garlic
2 teaspoons ground cumin
½ teaspoon salt
¼ teaspoon cayenne pepper
1 tablespoon dried dill

In a food processor or blender, combine everything up to the dill, processing until smooth. Add more water if you need to for desired smoothness. Add the dill, pulse a few times until distributed, taste and adjust seasonings.

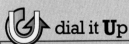 dial it **Up**

Add a tablespoon or two of olive oil to make it richer and more like a traditional hummus.

Mains
Asparagus and Potato Casserole

I enjoy cooking from scratch but I also love easy little conveniences that don't compromise the recipe, which is why this dish features frozen potatoes. Baked until tender in an eggy, custardy, vaguely Hollandaise-like sauce, this flavorful dish may become one of your weekend standards. This filling - but oil-free - casserole hits the spot on a weekend when you're craving something more substantial than toast and coffee. Don't let the long list of ingredients freak you out: it's easy and affordable to make and it makes a large amount. It's also great for a brunch with friends or leftovers. It's very adaptable: if you have a craving for different veggies and herbs, throw those in. Served with hot sauce on the side, this hearty casserole is the quintessential comfort food.

Creamy Sauce

1¼ cup plain, unsweetened nondairy milk
⅓ cup raw cashews or cashew pieces
¼ cup nutritional yeast
1 teaspoon garlic powder
1 cup firm silken tofu
½ teaspoon turmeric

1 teaspoon salt
1 teaspoon baking powder
1 teaspoon onion powder
2 tablespoons garbanzo bean flour
1 tablespoon fresh lemon juice
Pinch of cayenne powder
Pinch black salt powder

Casserole

$^1/_3$ cup low-sodium vegetable broth or 1 tablespoon neutral oil, like olive oil
$^2/_3$ cup shallots, diced
10-ounce super-firm or pressed tofu
1 tablespoon low-sodium tamari
20-oz. frozen roasted potatoes

12-oz. fresh or frozen asparagus, cut in 1-inch pieces
1 cup salsa
2 tablespoons dried dill weed
2 tablespoons fresh chives, minced
Smoked paprika
Ground pepper

Preheat the oven to 350 degrees. Line a 9-X-13-inch pan with parchment paper.

Blend the Creamy Sauce mixture until smooth.

In a large skillet on medium heat, sauté shallots for five minutes, stirring often, adding more broth if needed. Add the tofu and tamari, cook for 3 - 4 minutes. Add the frozen potatoes, stir through with a spatula, and add asparagus, salsa and dill. Pour eggy sauce over the top and cook, stirring often, for about 5 minutes. Transfer to the prepared pan, smooth flat, sprinkle with paprika, pepper and minced chives. Cover with foil, bake for 45 minutes, remove the foil and bake ten minutes more. Serve warm.

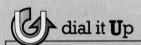 dial it **U**p

Sprinkle with vegan cheddar over the top after removing the foil and return to oven for 10 minutes.

Didja Know?

The Easter story of an egg-laying bunny named Osterhase is believed to have been brought to the US by German immigrants in the 18th century. Children would make nests for the colorful eggs and eventually, the nests evolved into baskets.

Desserts
Filled Chocolate Easter Eggs

Because there is nothing that fills a void in my Jewess heart more than conquering gentile foods, I present to you my recipe for Filled Chocolate Easter Eggs. Rich, decadent and a wee bit naughty, these chocolate eggs can be molded around any number of tasty fillings, from ganache to caramel, but here I've used vegan marshmallows (<u>Dandies</u> brand, to be exact) for a really low-effort egg with maximum pizazz or peanut butter, which is a wee bit more effort (not much, honestly) and tastes like a peanut butter cup in egg form. Bite into one and it's so goyishe, you'll practically hear Judy Garland singing Easter Parade in the background. Eggs are an enduring symbol of spring, reminding us of everything coming back to life after a long winter and if we can have our eggs without harming or exploiting others, it's all the better. I recommend a silicone egg mold because they are very easy to work with; I found mine at Michael's craft store.

Chocolate
20 oz. slavery-free, vegan chocolate chips, reserving about ½ cup (see page 43)
1 tablespoon coconut oil

Place a heatproof bowl over a small saucepan of simmering water and add the chocolate chips (except the reserved ½ cup) and coconut oil. Stir until the chocolate is nearly melted, carefully remove from the saucepan, and add the remaining chocolate chips. Stir until melted.

You will want to use something like a cutting board under your silicon egg mold to keep it stable and flat as you transport it to your fridge for setting.

151

Filled Chocolate
Easter Eggs
(cont.)

With the melted chocolate, use the back of a small spoon to coat every part of the interior of each egg shape. Make sure there are no areas missing chocolate. Place the mold in your fridge for about 25 minutes or until set.

Meanwhile, prepare your fillings.

Peanut Butter Filling

½ **cup smooth peanut butter**
¼ **cup organic powdered sugar, sifted**
2 teaspoons pure vanilla extract
¼ **teaspoon salt**

Heat, stirring over double-boiler with simmering water until the filling is thick and fully mixed. Allow to cool.

Marshmallow Filling

6 regular size vegan marshmallows or 12 minis

Full size marshmallows will likely be wider than the cavity of your egg mold and may bump out of the bottom a little. It won't effect the pretty top surface, though. If this bothers you, slice the marshmallows a little smaller with a sharp knife. I didn't care so I left them alone.

Remove the set egg bottoms from the fridge.

If using the peanut butter filling, roll ½ tablespoon of peanut butter filling in your hands and insert in the middle of each egg shape. Using a spoon, top with melted chocolate. If using the marshmallows, simply place in each egg shape and cover with chocolate. A little messy and a lot of fun.

Put in the fridge until set, about one hour. Serve at room temperature. If you have extra chocolate and marshmallows, dip 'em in chocolate and enjoy. I won't tell anyone.

Which beans are in the best shape?

Runner beans.

Carrot Cake
with Cashew Cream Frosting

Since I found a bunch of food processor blades at a resale shop, I have found that I no longer dread shredding veggies. One, two, three, done. Latkes? Easy peasy. Carrot cake? Same thing. Even without a shredding blade or even a food processor, though, this carrot cake is more than worth the effort. Fluffy, succulent, full of aromatic spices and sweet carrots, this cake manages to be a whole food treat without tasting like it.

The VeganEgg adds a rich depth of flavor so I highly recommend using it. Don't be scared by the long list of ingredients: this is an easy and affordable cake.

Cake
1½ **cups all-purpose gluten-free flour blend**
1 **teaspoon baking soda**
1 **teaspoon baking powder**
½ **teaspoon xanthan gum** (optional but recommended)
½ **tablespoon pure vanilla extract**
2 **tablespoons unsweetened applesauce**
2 **teaspoons ground cinnamon**
½ **teaspoon ground nutmeg**
¼ **teaspoon ground ginger**
⅛ **teaspoon ground cardamom**

$^1/_8$ **teaspoon salt**
1 cup real maple syrup
1 prepared VeganEgg (2 tablespoons VeganEgg powder + ½ cup ice cold water)
½ cup raisins or dried fruit of preference
½ cup toasted pecans or nuts of preference
2 cups shredded carrots (this was about four medium carrots for me)

Cashew Cream Frosting
1 cup raw cashews, soaked in two cups water for an hour and drained
2 tablespoons plain, non-dairy milk
3 tablespoons maple syrup
1 teaspoon pure vanilla extract
2 tablespoons softened refined coconut oil (optional)

Begin soaking your cashews.

Preheat your oven to 350 degrees. Line a 9-x-13-inch baking pan with parchment paper or lightly oil.

In a large bowl, sift or whisk together the flour, baking soda, baking powder, xanthan gum, cinnamon, nutmeg, ginger, cardamom and salt. Then mix in the maple syrup, vanilla, applesauce and VeganEgg. Mix until almost combined, then add the raisins, pecans and carrots, folding until fully mixed. I find using a silicone spatula/scraper works great for this.

Bake for 23 minutes. Allow to cool.

While cooling, making your frosting by combining all the ingredients in your blender. Blend on high until smooth.

When the cake is fully cooled, frost. Refrigerate until all is chilled, about an hour, cut and serve.

The Vegan Flavors of Mexican Food

Mexican Oregano

Chipotle and Adobo

Lime

Cocoa

Avocado

Epazote

Poblano

Chayote

Tomatillo

Arbol Pepper

Chili Powder

Tomato

Nopales

Cumin

VeganStreet.com

Cinco de Mayo

Ah, finally after a long winter, we can have some fun fresh produce again. Cinco de Mayo is a festive, spirited holiday and all the more reason to celebrate with good friends and great food. Should we get right to it?

Why did the lady return the guacamole to the grocery store?

It was just the pits.

Didja Know?

Cinco de Mayo is often thought to be Mexican Independence Day but it's not: the holiday celebrates the Mexican victory over an invading French fleet on May 5, 1862 at the Battle of Puebla. Despite being smaller and less well-equipped, the Mexican army led by General Ignacio Zaragoza won. It is speculated that if Mexico had not defeated the French in the Battle of Puebla, France would have established an empire in Mexico.

⭐ Horchata

An easy and very affordable drink to enjoy, horchata is a traditional milk alternative with origins in Latin America with the ingredients that vary by locale; often it is also made with condensed or regular dairy milk in addition to the non-dairy milk, though. Some versions are made with ground seeds and nuts but this one is inspired by the Mexican rice milk version, a favorite in our home. It requires a little time for soaking and is best prepared with a powerful blender and fine-mesh sieve but is so worth it. You can also use different kinds of rice but long grain white will give you the most traditional, sweet flavor.

1 cup long grain white rice
²/₃ cup blanched almonds
2 cinnamon sticks
8 cups water, divided
2 teaspoons pure vanilla extract
½ cup real maple syrup
½ cup almond milk

Soak the rice, almonds and cinnamon sticks overnight in four cups of water, covered in the refrigerator.

Drain the rice, snap the cinnamon sticks in half, and add to a blender with 4 cups of water. Blend on high until very smooth. This might take a few minutes depending on your blender. Place a fine-mesh sieve over a pitcher and pour it through to catch any residue. Press what remains on the sieve through with a spoon. Pour this back into the blender with vanilla, maple syrup and almond milk. Blend until fully integrated and serve over ice. Store in a covered container in the fridge for up to a week.

Cashew Queso

Looking for a thick, rich vegan cheese sauce for nachos, dipping or just making life that much better? Have I got a queso for you! Full of flavor, this oil-free sauce satisfies without the consequences of dairy because raw cashews, which have the highest starch content of any nut at 23 grams (most others are at zero or one grams of starch), thickens as it is heated, resulting in a smooth, rich cheese sauce. Steamed potatoes add to the silky texture and red bell pepper adds a tanginess. Ideally, this is made in a high-speed blender to get it the smoothest but if you don't have one, just blend longer using a regular blender.

1 cup plain, unsweetened non-dairy milk
1 cup raw cashews, soaked for an hour or until softened
²/₃ cup roasted red bell pepper
1 cup steamed, peeled white potatoes (I used Yukon)
¼ - ¹/₃ cup nutritional yeast
2 teaspoons minced garlic or garlic granules
1 teaspoon onion granules
½ - 1 teaspoon cayenne powder
½ teaspoon ground cumin
1 teaspoon salt
¼ teaspoon pepper
1 tablespoon fresh lemon juice
8-ounces chopped green chilies (optional)

Blend everything together except the lemon juice until smooth. Transfer to a medium pot and cook, stirring often, over medium heat until thickened. This should take only a few minutes. Once it's thick, turn off the heat, stir in the lemon juice, and adjust seasonings to taste. Add optional chopped green chilies. Serve warm.

Loaded Nachos

This isn't so much a recipe as it is instructions because once you have the queso, it is so easy and entirely customizable.

1 bag tortilla chips
½ recipe Cashew Queso, warm
Optional add-ons: black beans, veggie chili, cilantro, warm refried beans, marinated peppers, guacamole, vegan sour cream, olives, vegan chorizo, etc.

Spread the tortilla chips in a baking pan and pour warm queso over the top. Serve with whatever additional add-ons you like.

Didja Know?

Like St. Patrick's Day, Cinco de Mayo is a more raucous celebration in the U.S. than in its country of origin. In Mexico, it is not a national holiday though public schools are closed nationwide on May 5 and it is a state holiday in Puebla, where historic military reenactments, parades and commemorations are the order of the day.

Why did the maize not succeed as a comedian?

It's jokes were too corny.

Mains
Tofu Rancheros
with Smoky Tomato Sauce

Great for breakfast, lunch, dinner or that most resplendent of meals, brunch, Tofu Rancheros is nourishing, filling and delicious. With mild, egg-y tofu scramble and a smoky tomato sauce that is the perfect complement, you can modify as you like but for me, it's a complete meal with some garlicky greens and Spanish rice on the side. Look for black salt at an Indian market or online to bring in the sulfur-y characteristic of eggs and look for the deliciously smoky adobo sauce in the Mexican section of a grocery store: you can use the peppers for something else, like adding to a chili. There are quite a few ingredients here but it's all pretty inexpensive and quick to make.

Tofu Rancheros

½ teaspoon olive oil
1 cup yellow onion, diced
1 - 2 cups other veggies, diced
(I used mushrooms and bell peppers but anything you like also would work)
2 cloves garlic, minced

1 tablespoon low-sodium tamari
1 lb. extra-firm tofu
¼ cup low-sodium vegetable broth and ½ teaspoon turmeric, mixed together
1 tablespoon nutritional yeast
1 tablespoon dried oregano

1 teaspoon cumin powder
⅛ teaspoon black salt
(kala namak) (optional but
recommended)

½ teaspoon smoked paprika
¼ teaspoon chili powder
15 ounces vegan refried beans
Salt and pepper to taste

Heat a large skillet over medium heat for a minute, add the olive oil, and heat for another minute. Add the onion and cook for about five minutes. Add the other veggies and tamari, cooking until softened, about five or six more minutes. Crumble the tofu into the pan with your hands and add the broth and other seasonings, cooking about ten minutes, stirring often. Lower the heat to medium-low.

Smoky Tomato Sauce

5-ounces tomato sauce
½ tablespoon tomato paste
1 tablespoon adobo sauce (in
chipotle pepper can)

1 teaspoon cumin powder
⅛ teaspoon cayenne powder
Salt and pepper to taste

Assemble: heat the corn tortillas with a tablespoon or so of refried beans. Pile on some warm Tofu Rancheros, any other additions and Smoky Tomato Sauce. Plate with any other components of the meal and serve.

How could you tell that the vegetables weren't happy?

They were completely steamed.

Easy Mango Ice Treat

This tropics-flavored, refreshing iced confection takes a while to freeze but it's so quick and easy to make, you'll always want to have some on hand. An ice cream maker is not necessary but you will need a high-speed blender or patience with a regular blender.

2 cups full-fat coconut milk
2 ripe bananas, peeled and frozen
2 cups frozen mango
1 teaspoon pure vanilla extract

Allow to thaw for 5 - 10 minutes. Combine all ingredients in your blender with the coconut milk at the bottom by the blades. Turn on at a low speed and increase to high using the tamper as needed. Pour into a pie plate and freeze for a few hours. Thaw for about five minutes, scoop and serve.

Didja Know?
The California Avocado Commission estimates that 81 million pounds of avocados are eaten on Cinco de Mayo, most in the form of guacamole.

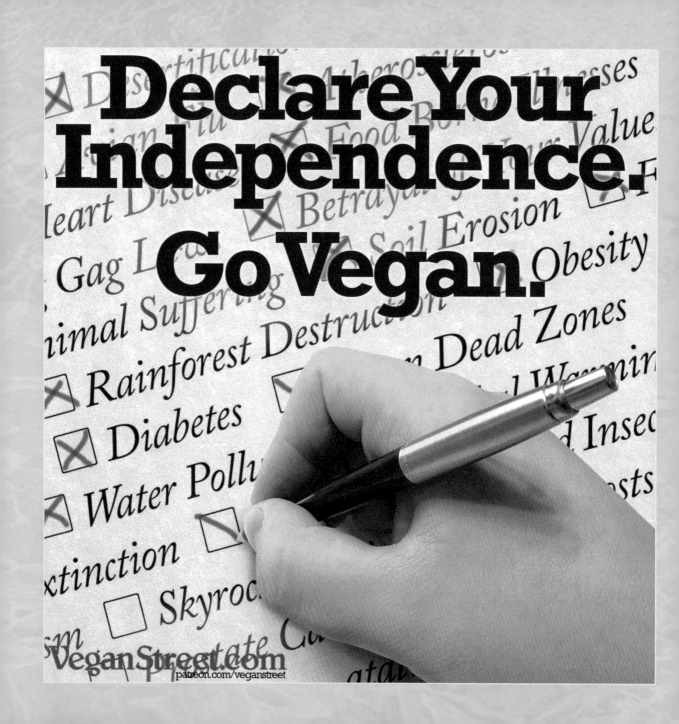

Fourth of July
and other summer shindigs

We go through a pretty intense winter here in Chicago so summer is precious to many of us, even the super-hot, humid days. Chicagoans are famous for using every opportunity when it's warm and dry to be outside, which is why we have so many street and culture festivals during the summer months and eating al fresco is such a fleeting special treat. When the sweet berries and melons are plentiful and farmers markets are bursting with produce at its peak, it's a great time to celebrate the juicy, fresh abundance plant foods in all their forms.

Why did the corn want to avoid the summer BBQ?

He didn't feel like being grilled.

This summer, let's do some

Grilling WITHOUT **Killing**

There are lots of great vegan burgers and sausages.

Slice up a crown of cauliflower, marinate it and toss it on the grill.

Grill up a stuffed pepper.

Slide all of your favorite vegetables onto skewers.

Photos: Tofurky Beer Brat – mrkate.com
Vegetarian Pelau-Stuffed Peppers – chow.com
Veggie Shish Kabob – food.com
Roasted Cauliflower Steaks – livebetteramerica.com

VeganStreet.com

169

Watermelon Chiller

Is there anything more delicious than cold, perfectly ripe watermelon on a hot summer day? In our region, full of intense winters and all-too-fleeting summers, watermelon is the very essence of summer. This makes it both bittersweet and deeply appreciated, especially as we get into peak watermelon season. With each one I buy, I think to myself, "This could very well be the last perfect watermelon of the season."

This treat is a highly accomplished one in that it manages to pull off being tangy, sweet, minty and refreshing in one glass. I promise that I won't do this often but this recipe does require a high-speed or at least a VERY good blender. (Perhaps it can be done in a food processor: I haven't checked.) Enjoy while the fireflies dance across your lawn; before too long, the leaves will be falling from the trees. Maybe if we drink enough of these, we can ward off winter altogether?

1 cup plain coconut water
½ fresh lime, squeezed
2 cups watermelon, cubed and frozen
1 frozen banana, peeled, chopped and frozen
1 tablespoon fresh mint

Add to a high-speed blender in the order listed. Blend until ready and enjoy!

What makes carrots among the most devoted plants?

They will almost always root for you.

Hummamole

What happens when you combine the best of hummus and the best of guacamole? You get the perfect sandwich or wrap spread. Combine creamy chickpea paste with silky avocado and you get the best of both worlds: familiar but with an intriguing twist, this is a protein-rich spread that is the perfect canvas for a nutritious veggie sandwich. If you want something that is a lower-fat substitute for guacamole, you can also use this, thinned out a bit with more water or lime juice.

15 ounces chickpeas, rinsed and drained (save dat bean water!)
1 ripe Hass avocado, cut into chunks
2 – 3 cloves garlic, minced or pressed
2 tablespoons fresh lime juice
2 tablespoons water
2 teaspoons ground cumin
1 teaspoon tamari
¼ teaspoon (or more) **cayenne** (optional)
Salt and fresh ground pepper to taste

Whirl together in a food processor until it is as smooth as desired. Spread on a sandwich or wrap.

Didja Know?
The word "solstice" is derived from the Latin words sol (sun) and sistere (to stand still), because the sun's relative position in the sky at noon does not appear to change much during the solstice.

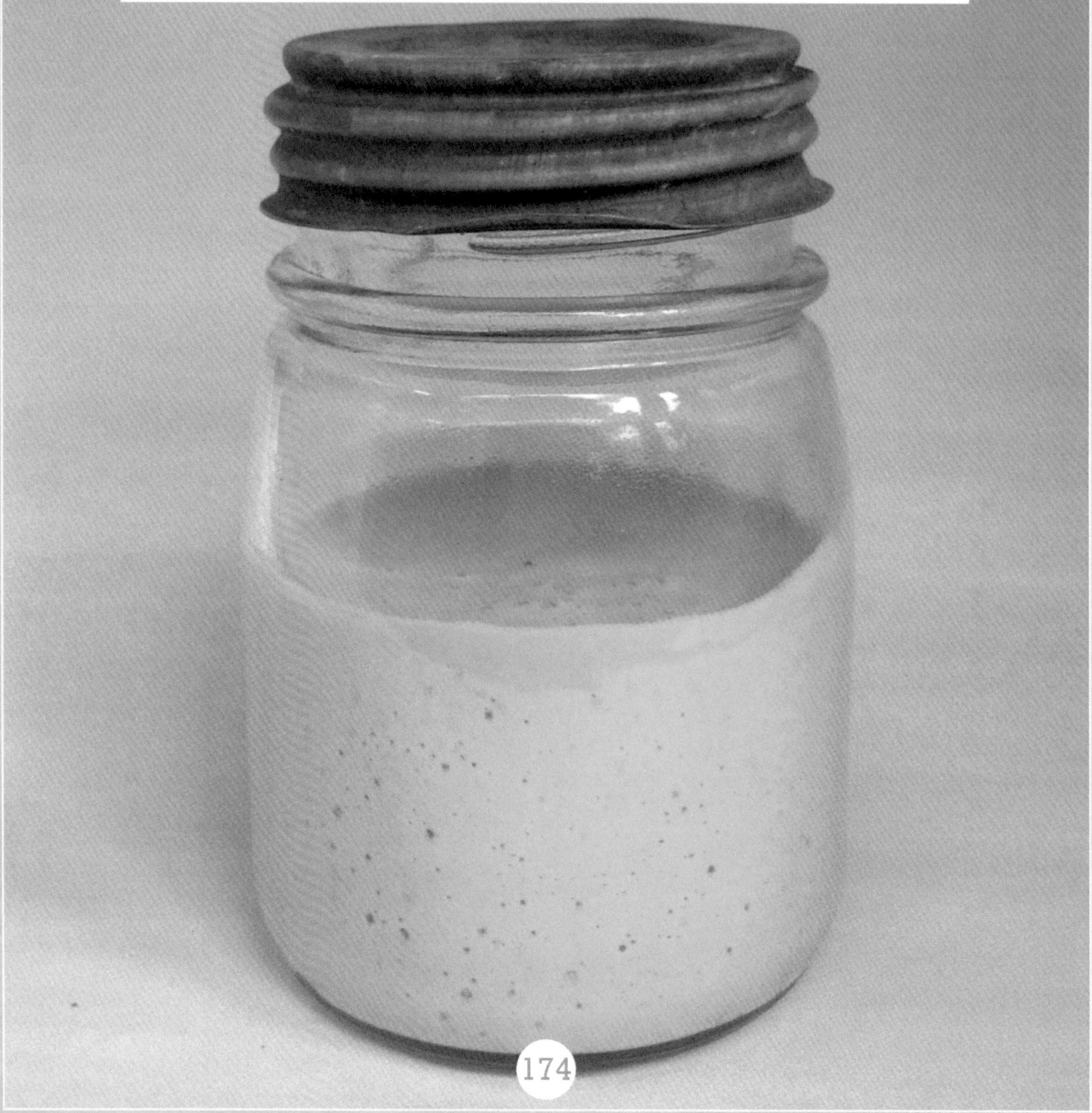

Green Goddess Dressing

This versatile dressing can be a pasta sauce, used in tacos, on salads, as a dip or any place you might use a pesto. With a bright, herb-y flavor and creamy texture, it's the perfect recipe to make any time of year but especially when it's summer and you don't want to heat up your kitchen and you can take the most advantage of fresh herbs. All you need is a knife, a chopping block, a blender and you're set! This will thicken in the fridge; if you want to thin it out, blend it up with a little water.

½ **cup raw cashews*, whole or pieces,**
½ **cup water**
½ **cup plain vegan yogurt**
1 cup flat-leaf parsley, chopped (stems removed)
3 tablespoons chives, minced
3 tablespoons fresh tarragon, minced
1 tablespoon nutritional yeast
1 tablespoon fresh lemon juice
1 tablespoon miso paste
1 teaspoon crushed garlic
¹/₈ teaspoon cayenne powder (optional)
Salt and pepper to taste

Blend until smooth. Serve.

* If you don't have a high-speed blender, consider soaking your cashews in hot water for about an hour to reach ideal smoothness.

Peach Bourbon BBQ Sauce

It was the box of organic peaches that first got me thinking about barbecue sauce. The peaches were perfection but some were dangerously close to ripeness so I wanted to use a lot of them at once. Freezing is always an option but I wanted something that was a little more immediate and fun. It wasn't long before the idea of BBQ sauce hit me. Peaches and bourbon: that's something people put together, right? In researching the topic, I learned that peach-bourbon BBQ sauce is indeed a southern culinary tradition.

As someone who doesn't have much tolerance for sweet sauces, this version is gently sweet while hitting all those other flavor nuances as well, creating a very balanced sauce with smoky, spicy, bitter and sour notes complementing the summer peach sweetness and keeping it from being cloying. This sauce can be tinkered with quite a bit, too, to emphasize and de-emphasize aspects of it. For example, if you like a spicier sauce, add more pepper and cayenne; if you prefer more sweet, you can add more maple syrup. For myself, because I do prefer to limit the sweetness, I used a ketchup brand that doesn't have sugar added. For me, the sauce is perfectly sweet without that but if you have regular ketchup that works just as well. It's all about tailoring it for your preference.

1 tablespoon olive oil or 1/3 cup low-sodium vegetable broth
1 cup Vidalia onion or other sweet onion, chopped
2 – 3 cloves garlic, minced
1 – 2 jalapeño peppers, seeds and pith removed
2 cups peeled and chopped fresh peaches, pits removed
1 cup ketchup
½ cup bourbon
⅓ cup pure maple syrup
⅓ cup apple cider vinegar
2 tablespoons molasses
2 tablespoons vegan Worcestershire sauce
1 tablespoon tamari
½ teaspoon dry mustard
½ teaspoon cayenne pepper
Salt and pepper to taste

In a large skillet, heat your olive oil or broth over medium heat for a minute. Add the onions, garlic and peppers and cook, stirring often, for about five minutes, until softened. (If using broth, you may need to add more by the tablespoon to keep it from sticking.) Add all the other ingredients and bring to a boil; lower the heat and cook over a medium-low heat and simmer for 25 minutes, stirring occasionally. When cool enough to handle, add to a blender and blend until smooth. This will store in the fridge for several weeks in an airtight container.

Which berries make the rudest audiences?

Raspberries.

Mains
Falafel Burgers

Oh, these burgers!

I am a big fan of falafel but I rarely eat it these days because it's hard to eat all that oil without feeling like I've swallowed a deep-fried hockey puck. I still love the flavors, though, and the protein boost that comes from my favorite plump little legume, the humble chickpea. Mashing up the familiar flavors of falafel with creamy tahini as the binder and we've got a patty that packs a great punch: the tang of lemon, the earthy-smoky spices and dense, buttery chickpeas all puréed together. Pair this burger with homemade harissa, the classic spicy Tunisian chili purée, cooling cucumbers and a squiggle of tahini sauce and you've got a burger that hits all the right notes. Warning: these did not work on the grill – too fragile and sticky – but if you don't want to bake them, they would probably work in a lightly oiled skillet just fine.

(Makes four large burgers)

15 oz. cooked chickpeas, drained and rinsed
½ cup onion, generous
⅓ cup tahini
3 cloves garlic, minced
2 tablespoons chickpea flour or flour of your choice
1½ tablespoons fresh lemon juice
½ teaspoon salt, ground pepper to taste
1 teaspoon coriander
1 teaspoon cumin
¼ teaspoon cayenne

Falafel Burgers
(cont.)

Process all the above ingredients in a food processor until well-mixed, a minute or two. It can have some texture. Process longer for smoother patties. If it clumps together in the food processor, smooth it out with a spoon. Refrigerate the "batter" for at least one hour to firm.

Preheat the oven to 375 degrees.

Using a scooper (an ice cream scoop worked best for me), place four burgers on a parchment-lined baking sheet. This is fairly sticky stuff, so having a second spoon for scooping out and damp hands for shaping helped. Bake for 16 minutes, carefully flip with a spatula and bake for 13 more minutes. They are ready to eat.

Before making the burgers, start your harissa paste.

Harissa paste
4 oz. dried chiles (I used a combination of guajillo and arbol peppers)
Boiling water
4 cloves garlic, minced
1 teaspoon ground caraway
1 teaspoon ground cumin seed
1 teaspoon ground coriander seed
½ teaspoon salt
2 tablespoons olive oil
1 - 2 tablespoons reserved soaking water

Place the chiles in a heat-proof bowl and cover with hot water, then cover the bowl. Let this sit for 30 minutes, then remove the steams and seeds from your softened chiles. (Reserve a little soaking liquid for thinning out your paste.) Gloves are helpful here! No matter what, though, don't touch your eyes without washing your hands thoroughly. You don't need to remove all the seeds.

Place the chiles in your food processor along with the rest of the ingredients except for the olive oil and soaking water. Make a chunky paste by pulsing together. With the food processor running, trickle in the olive oil. Scrape down the bowl of your food processor as necessary, and add a little reserved soaking water until you get the texture you want.

This paste can be stored in an airtight container in the refrigerator for up to a month with a thin layer of olive oil on top to preserve freshness.

Tahini Sauce
¼ cup tahini
Juice of ½ lemon
Water

In a cup, mix together the tahini and lemon juice until you have a thick paste. Add water a little at a time until you reach the desired thinness.

Toast your bun or pita bread.

Garnish with: **Cucumber Tomatoes Romaine Lettuce Red Onion**

Place a thin layer of harissa, then the falafel burger, then the veggies you like (cucumbers and tomatoes are a classic combination with falafel), and a squiggle of tahini sauce.

Baked Corn Dogs

Who doesn't love a corn dog? Crispy, carb-y and decadent, corn dogs bring to mind summer, carnivals and simple pleasures but they come with a lot of baggage: corn dogs are crispy because they're deep-fried – mmm, fried deliciousness – and that's something many of us try to avoid, both because of the messy kitchen and the empty calorie gut bomb. These corn dogs take the rich, flavorful batter – the taste boosted with actual corn – and, with a fraction of the oil, result in a satisfying, comfort food with a much-improved nutritional profile.

6 corn dog sticks or wooden skewers
6 jumbo vegan hot dogs, cooked and cooled
½ cup plain, unsweetened plant-based milk
¼ cup aquafaba (see page 107)
1 teaspoon fresh lemon juice
4 teaspoons maple syrup

³/₄ cup frozen corn, defrosted
1½ cups gluten-free, all-purpose flour
1 cup fine cornmeal
1 teaspoon onion powder
¼ teaspoon cayenne powder

Why was the tomato sauce frustrated?

It felt it could never ketchup.

¼ teaspoon xanthan gum
Salt and pepper to taste
2 tablespoons refined coconut oil or vegan butter, solid

Preheat the oven to 375 degrees. Line a cookie sheet with parchment paper.

Combine the milk, aquafaba, lemon juice, maple syrup and corn in a blender and blend until smooth.

In a large bowl, combine the flour, cornmeal, onion powder, cayenne powder, xanthan gum, salt and pepper. Cut in the oil or vegan butter and mix into the flour with a fork. Stir in the milk and mix with a spoon until it comes together. It should stick between your fingers. If it is too dry, add more milk or oil; if it is too wet, add more flour. It needs to coat and stick to your veggie dogs. Mix until combined. It should be thick but smooth.

Take a handful of better and shape around the veggie dogs. It is very forgiving dough. Keep molding until the entire veggie dog is covered and in the shape of a corn dog. Prepare all the dogs and then push in your sticks. Place on your baking sheet.

Bake for ten minutes, flip and bake for ten minutes more, so 20 minutes total, until golden on both sides. Serve with mustard, ketchup, cashew cheese or whatever you like!

Which fruits don't give you enough space?

Cling peaches.

Barbecue Tofu Salad
with Cashew Ranch Dressing

Summer is a great time for salads, of course, and if you want to boost the protein and make it more of a substantial meal, you could make a tasty salad like this one. Tofu was just what I used: chickpeas, seitan and other meatless proteins would work just as well. I used super-firm tofu, the kind that is getting easier to find these days but still not as common as the water-packed varieties. You can find it at Whole Foods and Trader Joe's in the refrigerated section with the other tofu. What makes it different is it is super-dense and firm without needing to be pressed. Personally, I love the organic Wildwood High-Protein super-firm variety. For those seeking tofu that doesn't have that weird sponginess, this is the one for you. Cook it up with a little BBQ sauce and serve in a salad along with some zingy Cashew Ranch and you will not be disappointed.

20-ounces super-firm tofu or vegan protein of your choice
1 cup Peach-Bourbon Barbecue sauce (see page 176)
or your BBQ sauce of choice

Salad fixings (I used romaine, red onion, carrot, cucumber and toasted corn tortillas)

In a medium skillet, heat to medium-high, and add the tofu and BBQ sauce. Bring to a hard simmer and lower to medium-low, cooking for 25 minutes and stirring occasionally.

Make your Cashew Ranch Dressing or use a store-bought vegan ranch or dressing of choice.

Cashew Ranch Dressing

1 cup cashews, soaked for an hour or more and drained
3/4 cup water
1 tablespoon fresh lemon juice
1 teaspoon garlic granules
1 tablespoon nutritional yeast
Salt and pepper to taste

Place the ingredients in a blender and blend until smooth.

Compose or mix your salad. Place the BBQ tofu on top and serve with Cashew Ranch Dressing.

Didja Know?

In Ancient Egypt, the summer solstice preceded the appearance of the Sirius star, which the Egyptians believed was responsible for the annual flooding of the Nile and essential to their agriculture. Because of this, the Egyptian calendar was set so that the start of the year coincided with the appearance of Sirius, just after the solstice. In fact, it was the ancient Romans who noticed that Sirius, thought of as the "nose" of the constellation Canis Major and also known as the Dog Star, happened to rise and fall with the sun during late July through August, which is why that time of year is referred to as the "dog days" of summer.

186

Peanut Butter Dream Freezer Pie

Why this expression, easy as pie? Given the choice, I would make bars, cookies or even cakes over pie any day. It's not that I don't like pie. I'm just not so talented with making pie crusts that don't taste like flattened cardboard. Anything involving the rolling out of dough, in fact, finds me panicked and tense.

Who doesn't love a good pie, though? Determined to get over my anxiety about pie crusts, I worked one out that works great for the luscious, silky filling and requires no rolling pins. Press into place and, voilà, pie crust!

This is truly easy as pie to make. With a rich, smooth ganache over a creamy, peanut butteriffic filling and a naturally sweet crust, this is a perfect treat reminiscent of ice cream pie, ideal for dinner guests, summer parties, and just enjoying on a piece-by-piece basis. The pie keeps getting better the longer it sits in the freezer but, if you are like me, you won't be able to test this out for too many days.

Crust
2 cups pecans
¾ cup medjool dates, pitted
1 tablespoon slavery-free vegan cacao or cocoa powder (see page 43)
1 teaspoon pure vanilla extract
¼ teaspoon salt

Pulse the pecans in a food processor until you get fine crumbs, about ten pulses. Add the rest of the ingredients and process until fully mixed.

Peanut Butter Pie
(cont.)

Press into the bottom of a 9- or 10-inch springform or regular pie plate.

Peanut Butter Filling
2 cups (1 pint) vegan creamer (I used So Delicious Original Coconut creamer)
1 cup organic powdered sugar
1 tablespoon vanilla extract
1 ½ tablespoon arrowroot mixed in a small cup with 2 tablespoons plain non-dairy milk (I used almond)
½ cup smooth peanut butter
½ teaspoon cardamom (optional)
¼ teaspoon salt

Blend together in blender until smooth and then pour over the prepared crust. Leave in the freezer for 3 - 4 hours until set.

When firm, prepare your ganache.

Ganache
1 ½ cups slavery-free vegan chocolate chips (see page 43) **or finely chopped chocolate bar**

½ cup vegan creamer
(I used the same as above: So Delicious Original Coconut)
1 teaspoon pure vanilla extract

Put the chocolate chips in a medium heat-proof bowl. Heat the creamer in a small saucepan over medium-high until beginning to simmer. Pour over the chocolate chips along with the vanilla and cover with a bowl. Let it sit for a few minutes, then whisk until smooth.

Pour over the frozen peanut butter layer and smooth out with a spoon. Freeze for an additional hour or two. Enjoy!

*I used pecan pieces because they are less expensive than whole pecans and get ground up anyway.

Fourth of July Fruit Skewers

With a citrus-y glaze that brightens the flavor and keeps the bananas from getting brown, this is the perfect healthy treat to create with little hands, and it's so much fun to see the flag start to take shape. No matter your country of origin, you can turn delectable fruit into a fun, edible representation of your national flag.

I used one half-pint of blueberries, 1 pint of raspberries (simply because those were more likely to have been crushed at the bottom) and 4 - 5 bananas. I used thirteen skewers - four had seven blueberries, and then three banana slices alternating with three raspberries; three had four blueberries alternating with three slices of banana, plus three more slices of banana alternating with three raspberries; the last six were all alternating raspberries and banana slices for the stripes. You could also decide to use other fruit, for example strawberries, cherries, or blackberries.

Last, I used an agave-lime glaze to keep the bananas from turning brown. I brushed it on after the skewers were put together.

Four Agave Lime Glaze
2 tablespoons lime juice
2 tablespoons agave nectar

Mix with a spoon and gently brush over the skewers. If you have any leftover liquid, add some ice and water for an instant limeade.

Serving suggestions: Eat off the skewer herbivore caveman style or dip the fruit in vegan yogurt or pudding. Enjoy!

Rainbow Pudding Parfait

One of the biggest summer events here in Chicago is the annual Pride Parade. I created this recipe to celebrate the legalization of gay marriage. The rainbow flag is a symbol of the LGBTQ community and aren't colorful foods also great for us to eat? Put those two together in this summery recipe and you have a perfect treat for any day you want to celebrate justice, liberty, progress and fruit-y deliciousness in lovely parfait form. You can use any vegan pudding, though I think a neutral color works best, and whatever purple, blue, green, yellow, orange and red fruits you like. We used two 24-ounce Ball jars to be able to fit everything in here but this would also be pretty in a single medium glass bowl.

½ **cup organic cornstarch**
½ **cup organic sugar**
¼ **teaspoon salt**
¼ **teaspoon ground nutmeg**
3 cups unsweetened non-dairy milk (we used almond)
1 teaspoon pure vanilla extract

In a medium saucepan, whisk together the cornstarch, sugar, salt and nutmeg. Turn the heat to medium and slowly add your milk and vanilla. Whisk frequently until the mixture has thickened, about ten minutes.

Once thickened, allow to cool for ten minutes or so, then transfer to a covered dish and chill for three hours or more.

Take the pudding out and bring to room temperature. Stir vigorously to get your pudding smooth again. Meanwhile, prepare your fruit. Get your Ball jars and start layering, beginning and ending with fruit. We used red grapes for purple, blueberries for blue, kiwi for green, pineapple for yellow, mango for orange (though cantaloupe might have been more orange-y to contrast better with the pineapple) and strawberries. Eat right after layering or chill and enjoy.

Didja Know?

The peaceful three-hour Pan-European Picnic was held on August 19, 1989 at the border gates of Austria and Hungary. This picnic was part of the Revolutions of 1989 and considered a crucial milestone that led to the reunification of East and West Germany and the lifting of the Iron Curtain. The picnic site is commemorated with monuments today.

Not everyone enjoys fireworks.

Loud explosions and flashing lights are very frightening to a lot of animals. Keep your pets in quiet indoor rooms when there are fireworks nearby.

Photo: 2ndhandbarking.com

VeganStreet.com

Fireworks Safety

I love summer but I really am not a fan of fireworks and neither are any of our three companion animals, who pretty much go into hiding during the days around July 4. I know they are not alone. Here are some ways to keep your animals safe and a bit less stressed during the summer fireworks season…

• Do not leave them in your yard unattended. They could get spooked and escape, getting lost and becoming exposed to danger. According to the ASPCA, there is an uptick in lost dogs and cats around July 4. Keep them safe and sound indoors.

• Products like ThunderShirts, which help to reduce anxiety by applying gentle pressure, can be used on both dogs and cats.

• Even if you keep your cats indoors, consider having them wear a collar with tags during July 4 in case they bolt during the stress of the fireworks.

• Do not take your dogs to fireworks displays. It is just not enjoyable.

• Give your dogs plenty of walks and potty time before the fireworks.

• If you have especially fearful companion animals, create a quiet, den-like environment for them in a room with the windows and shades down. Some dogs feel calmer in crates. Give them this option. Make sure that ample water is available, of course, if they are closed off.

HAPPY VEGANNIVERSARY

with Love, from All the Animals

VeganStreet.com

Veganniversary

One of my favorite days of the year is February 1 because even though it's usually pretty cold and dreary in Chicagoland, that was the date in 1995 that John and I went vegan. I consider the decision to the best choice I ever made. (Even better than stopping my practice of dating undeserving dudes.) When we celebrated our tenth veganniversary, we got a big cake from the Chicago Diner and had a party with lots of friends. (I thought I was so clever in having them write "Happy Veganniversary" on the cake but now it is part of the common parlance among vegans.) Your veganniversary, whenever it is, is a time to celebrate being on the right side of history and take pride in the fact that you are part of a phenomenal movement of people who are changing the world for the better. Plus you can hang out with cows and chickens without feeling any guilt. What better way to celebrate than to enjoy some fabulous vegan food with friends? Consider doing a fundraising drive for the compassionate charity of your choice to commemorate your next veganniversary.

How many vegans does it take to screw in a light bulb?

Two. One to screw it in and the other to check for animal ingredients.

Happy Veganniversary, Darling

VeganStreet.com

Tropical Green Shake

I developed this recipe when I was intoxicated by some beautiful spring days that got me in the mood for something a little tangy, sweet and creamy. The spinach gives it a little extra nutritional boost. This drink hits all the right notes, creating something you might sip on the beach in Negril or even your own back yard when you want to get away from it all. This is also perfect for a spring or summer brunch and pretty with some fresh mint on top.

3 dates, soaked in hot water for ten minutes and pitted
½ ripe avocado
1 – 2 oranges, mandarins or tangelos, peeled
Juice from ½ lime
1 cup spinach
1 cup frozen mango
1½ cups water or coconut water
5 – 6 ice cubes

Mix with a spoon and gently brush over the skewers. If you have any leftover liquid, add some ice and water for an instant limeade.

Serving suggestions: Eat off the skewer herbivore caveman style or dip the fruit in vegan yogurt or pudding.

Onion Dill Dip

Perfect for any time of year, this luscious dip provides an exceptional reason to eat more celery and carrot sticks, and, well, you can even stick some potato chips in it and I won't tell. Soy- and oil-free, this Onion-Dill Dip relies on cashews and beans for its creaminess and while it's quite a bit lighter than most similar dips – even vegan ones – there is no sacrifice of flavor or indulgent texture. With great salty-sour and onion-y notes, this will probably not be a dip you'll want to eat right before kissing under the mistletoe but it will have your officemates at the company holiday party wondering how the heck a vegan did this. Explain your sorcery, herbivore! Smile and hand them the recipe. If you don't mind the calories and you want to make it taste a bit more like a traditional onion dip, substitute one of the excellent vegan mayos on the market for the beans.

Don't let the long list of ingredients alarm you: most are pantry items and easy to buy in small amounts in the bulk section of a natural foods store. It is also something you can make with a minimum of effort. A high-speed blender works best for creating a smooth cashew base but you can achieve this with a regular blender or even food processor and a bit of patience.

1 heaping cup raw cashews*, soaked for 4 hours or more and drained
½ cup water

½ **cup white beans** (I used Great Northern, but navy or cannellini would also be great), **drained and rinsed**
2 tablespoons plain, unsweetened vegan milk (I used almond)
2 teaspoons apple cider vinegar or fresh lemon juice
1 – 2 teaspoons tamari
3 tablespoons nutritional yeast
2 tablespoons dried dill
1½ tablespoons dried minced onion
1 teaspoon garlic granules
1 teaspoon onion granules
Salt and pepper to taste
1 – 2 tablespoons minced chives

Place your drained cashews in a blender along with ½ cup of water. Blend, using your tamper, until smooth, about a minute. Add your beans, milk, apple cider vinegar, tamari and nutritional yeast. Blend until it is smooth and creamy. Pulse in the rest of your ingredients, not including the chives. Stir with a spoon, transfer to the bowl you will be serving this in, and sprinkle the minced chives on top. Cover and allow to chill for two or more hours before serving.

*I recommend using cashew pieces, as they tend to be less expensive than whole ones and they will be ground up anyway.

Why did the vegan cheese have an inferiority complex?

It felt it wasn't gouda-nough.

Gateway Vegan Lasagna

I have long tried to create that perfect comfort lasagna that anyone would enjoy. This lasagna is the result of that quest. Over the years, I've finessed and tinkered with things to arrive at this, what I call my Gateway Vegan Lasagna. Why gateway? I have brought this lasagna to many gatherings with meat-eaters and it is gobbled up faster than you can say, "Fooled ya." With a deliciously savory marinara and a luscious, rich spinach spread that could double for a dip, this lasagna is not going to be mistaken for health food any time soon and there's a good reason for that: it's not, though it is full of a good amount of veggies. This lasagna intended to be a vegan gateway in casserole form. Omnis cannot believe it's vegan.

Fungi haters can feel free to sub anything for the mushrooms or skip altogether but a juicy sautéed veggie is good here: eggplant, red bell peppers, etc. Also feel free to add vegan sausages with the sauté or use your favorite cashew cheese on top. Don't let the long ingredient's list intimidate you: it is affordable to make and quite easy, though, like most lasagna, will take a bit of time. It is worth every minute.

1 tablespoon olive oil, plus any for lightly oiling your pan
1 yellow onion, diced
3 cloves garlic, minced
8-ounces baby bella or mushrooms of choice (optional**) or veggies you prefer**
1 teaspoon oregano
1 teaspoon fennel
1 teaspoon oregano

Gateway Vegan Lasagna (cont.)

½ teaspoon crushed red pepper
28-ounces crushed tomatoes
1 cup low-sodium vegetable broth
12⅓ ounces firm silken tofu
16-ounces frozen spinach,
defrosted and water squeezed out
1 cup fresh basil, packed
½ cup plus 2 tablespoons vegan mayo
4 tablespoons nutritional yeast
1 teaspoon garlic granules
1 teaspoon onion granules
1 teaspoon fresh lemon juice
Salt and pepper to taste
12 no-boil lasagna noodles
1 cup shredded vegan mozzarella cheese, commercial or homemade

Preheat your oven to 350 degrees. Lightly oil a 9-x-13-inch rectangular baking pan.

In a large skillet, heat the olive oil over medium-high heat for a minute. Add the onions, garlic, fennel seeds, red pepper flakes and cook until onions soften and lightly brown, about five minutes. Add the mushrooms and sauté six minutes. Add the crushed tomatoes and broth. Cook until it begins to simmer and then lower the heat to medium-low. Cook here at a low simmer for 15 minutes.

In a food processor, add the tofu, basil, spinach, mayo, garlic and onion granules and lemon juice. Process until smooth, and season to taste with salt and pepper.

In your prepared pan, cover the bottom with tomato sauce. Top with four noodles (I had three going horizontal and one vertical to cover the space). Cover the noodles with one-third the spinach mixture. Cover the spinach mixture with one-third the sauce. Layer again exactly the same: four noodles, the one-third the spinach mixture, then one-third of the sauce. Do this one more time with the remaining noodles, spinach blend and sauce. Cover with aluminum foil and bake for 45 minutes. Remove the foil, sprinkle with cheese, and bake about 15 more minutes.

Allow to sit for 10 minutes, cut into squares and serve.

Didja Know?

The first known vegan was Syrian-born blind poet and philosopher Al-Ma'arri, who was born in 973. In his later years, Al-Ma'arri wrote:
*Do not unjustly eat fish
the water has given up,
And do not desire as food
the flesh of slaughtered animals,
Or the white milk of mothers
who intended its pure draught
for their young, not noble ladies.
And do not grieve the unsuspecting
birds by taking eggs;
for injustice is the worst of crimes.
And spare the honey which the bees
get industriously from the flowers
of fragrant plants;
For they did not store it
that it might belong to others,
Nor did they gather it for bounty
and gifts.
I washed my hands of all this;
and wish that I
Perceived my way before
my hair went gray!"*

Loaded Baked Potatoes

Sometimes, you just have to go for it. Especially when it's cold out, we are seeking our creature comforts and I don't know if anything comes as close as these warming baked potatoes with their indulgent-tasting, savory sauce. Made without any oil, they are still deliciously creamy and comforting, not sacrificing taste at all despite their nutritious profile. A great side dish or light meal, these Loaded Baked Potatoes are highly adaptive to whatever toppings you might like. Give them a try – you may just find yourself licking the plate clean.

4 – 6 russet potatoes, baked

Cheesy sauce

2 - 3 cloves garlic, minced
½ cup gluten-free all-purpose blend
1 cup nutritional yeast
1 tablespoon dried dill weed
2 teaspoons onion powder
2 cups low-sodium vegetable stock
2 cups unsweetened plain non-dairy milk (I used almond)
1 tablespoon tamari
Salt and pepper to taste

1 bunch broccoli, cut into florets
15½ oz. cooked chickpeas, drained and rinsed
1 cup defrosted frozen peas
1 tablespoon lemon juice
1 bunch scallions, sliced

Optional topping additions: vegan bacon, red pepper flakes, dairy-free sour cream, salsa, etc.

In a medium mixing bowl, whisk the dry ingredients and then add the liquid, mixing together until the clumps are largely dissolved (some small ones are fine as they will break up as you cook it).

In a medium pot over medium heat, sauté the minced garlic in a couple of tablespoons of vegetable stock, stirring often to prevent burning. After three minutes or so, pour in the sauce you've already mixed, whisking frequently until beginning to bubble. Lower to medium low and cook, whisking often, until thickened.

Meanwhile, steam the broccoli until bright green.

Add the broccoli, defrosted peas and chickpeas to the cheesy sauce. Turn off heat, add lemon juice and season to taste.

Split your hot baked potatoes and top with the cheesy broccoli sauce. Sprinkle with chopped scallions and any additional toppings, like vegan bacon and pepper flakes.

Best Chocolate Cake

Known variously as Wacky Cake, Crazy Cake (don't yell at me, I didn't name it) and Depression Cake, this style of cake became popular during the 1930s but a version of it has been around since World War I and it was even sometimes known as War Cake. What made this cake popular then and why it remains so today is it results in a moist, rich chocolate cake without butter, eggs and milk, which were expensive and scarce for those on tight budgets. Thus this cake, relying on baking powder for eggs and vinegar to react to baking soda to produce carbon dioxide and give the batter a lift, was often vegan by default. Don't be afraid of the sharp acidity of the vinegar, by the way, as it will be undetectable in the finished cake. I have included a bit more options from the original recipe - cinnamon to make it extra lovely, raspberry jam in the middle, the options of vegan milk or coffee to add to the overall richness and, of course, frosting - but this cake will be perfectly delicious if you want to remain true to the original recipe and just make a plain chocolate cake with the water option. It's a fun cake to make with kids because it is so easy with such reliably good results. Does it need frosting? Not really but who doesn't want to gild the lily once in a while? It's your veganniversary, damn it! Top with Perfect Chocolate Frosting for the best cake yet.

3 cups all-purpose gluten-free flour (I used Bob's Red Mill 1-for-1 Baking Flour)

½ cup plus 2 tablespoons slavery-free cocoa powder (see page 43)

1½ cups granulated sugar (I used coconut sugar)

1 tablespoon baking powder

2 teaspoons ground cinnamon

1 teaspoon baking soda

1 teaspoon salt

1 teaspoon xanthan gum

12 tablespoons melted coconut oil or neutral oil of preference

1 tablespoon pure vanilla extract

2 cups plain, non-dairy milk, room temperature brewed coffee or cold water (or a combination)

2 tablespoons distilled white vinegar

¼ cup raspberry jam (if making a layer cake)

Preheat your oven to 325 degrees. Lightly oil a 9-X-13-inch pan, a bundt pan or two 8- or 9-inch cake pans.

Sift in the flour, cocoa powder, sugar, baking powder, cinnamon, baking soda and xanthan gum into a large mixing bowl. Make a well in the middle of the bowl and add the rest of the ingredients (not the jam). Stir together with a large, sturdy spoon until smooth. It will be thick.

Bake for 18 minutes. Turn and bake another 18 minutes or until when an inserted toothpick or cake tester comes out clean.

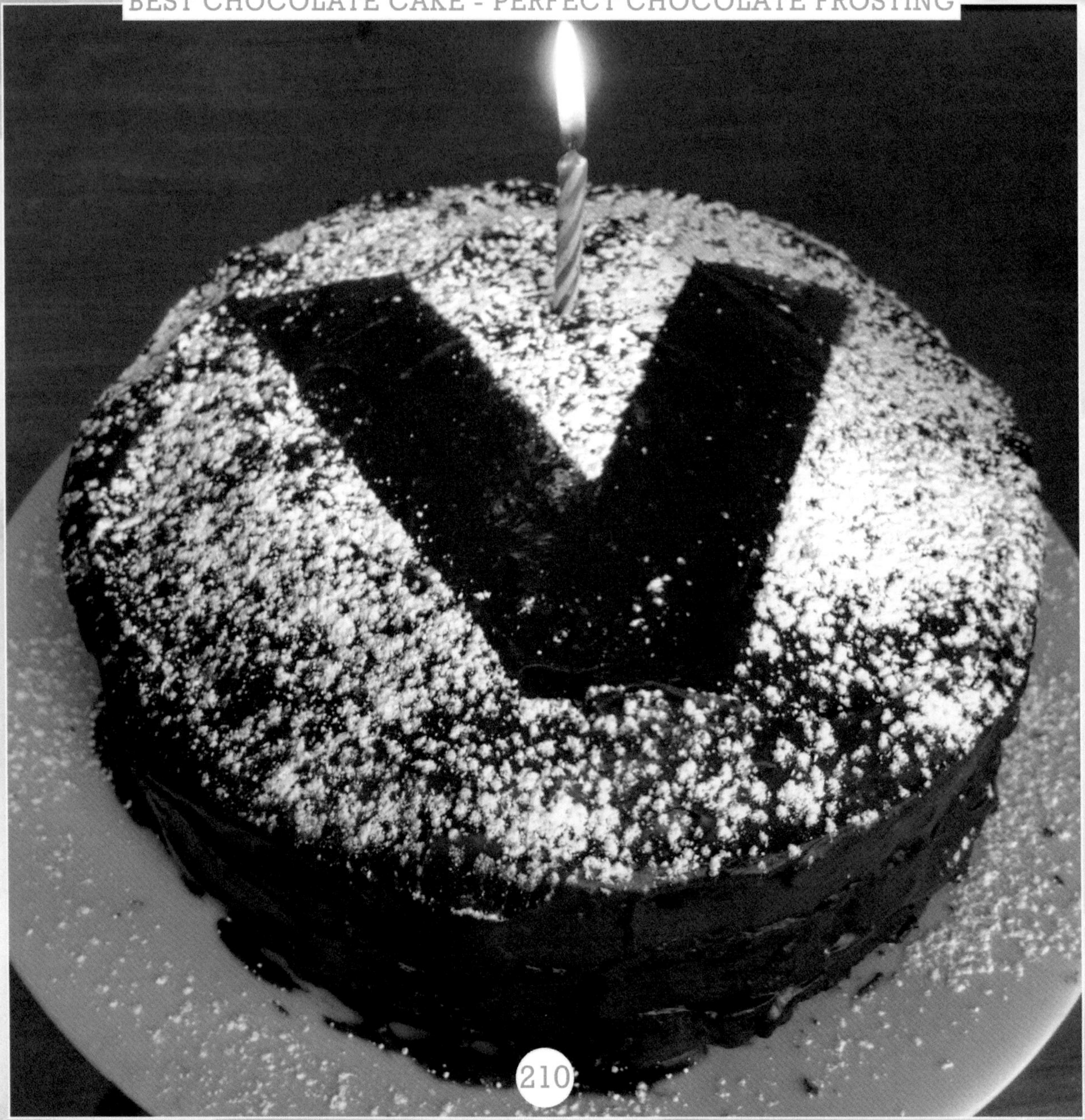

Perfect Chocolate Frosting

To spread over the Best Chocolate Cake, of course.

2 cups powdered sugar
¼ cup refined coconut oil
½ cup slavery-free cocoa powder (see page 43)
¼ cup plain, unsweetened nondairy milk
1 teaspoon pure vanilla extract
A dash of salt

In a stand mixer with the whisk attachment or with a hand mixer, combine the sugar and the coconut oil. Mix on medium for two minutes. Add the cocoa powder, milk and vanilla until smooth and thick, about two more minutes. Add a dash of salt. If it's too thick, add a little more milk by the tablespoon but don't thin it too much.

If you are frosting a two-layer cake, place one of the cakes, flat side down, on your cake stand or plate. Spoon the raspberry jam (from the Best Chocolate Cake recipe) over the top, leaving one inch around the edges so it doesn't smoosh out. Place the second cake on top of that domed - or top - side down, so the flat side is facing up. Gently press together. Frost the top and sides. Allow to chill in the refrigerator for 30 minutes or so and serve.

Happy veganniversary!

 Glam it up

Cut a "V" or another simple design out of cardboard or paper (or a paper plate) and use as a stencil for sifting powdered sugar over the top of a frosted cake. This is easiest with two people: one to hold the stencil and the other sifting.

Glam it up

For a layer cake, press crushed wafer cookies or candy sprinkles along the sides of the cake.

Solstices and Equinoxes

Solstices and equinoxes are deeply connected to seasons and that is something to celebrate. Solstices happen in the winter and the summer when the tilt of the Earth's axis reaches its maximum angle compared to the sun; the winter solstice marks the shortest day and longest night of the year, and summer is the longest day and shortest night. Equinoxes occur in the fall and spring, when Earth's axis is not tilted away or toward the sun, which results in a nearly equal amount of daytime and nighttime at all latitudes. Because of the connection to the natural cycle, solstices and equinoxes are a great time to celebrate with the foods and symbols of the seasons.

Winter Solstice

Occurring on December 21 or 22 in the Northern Hemisphere, winter solstice is a time of reflection, relaxation and time with loved ones. Holly, pine cones, evergreens and woodsy scents are especially appropriate for helping you to savor the season, and emphasizing the colors green, red and white can help to create a festive environment. Candles and fires, reminding us of the warm months ahead, are especially lovely. Nourishments to savor would be nogs, warm punches, nuts, cabbage, winter squashes, potatoes and other hearty root vegetables. Make the solstice more meaningful by donating to resale shops, giving monetary donations to the organizations you support, volunteering, making sure that wildlife have access to fresh water where you live, filling bird feeders and creating aromatic, simple homemade crafts like orange pomander balls studded with cloves.

I'm humming along to "River" by Joni Mitchell.

Spring (or Vernal) Equinox

Usually March 20 in the Northern Hemisphere, the spring equinox heralds the return to the warmth and new life. It's a time of rejoicing, renewed hope and shaking off the slumber of the winter months. Spending time outdoors and retiring some of your heavier winter blankets and darker furniture coverings will help to get you in the spirit of the lighter, brighter season. The traditional colors of the spring equinox are greens, yellows and pastels: give your home a little makeover with these pops of color here and there. Foods to enjoy are mint, chives, carrots, leeks, fava beans, peas, rhubarb, sprouts, salad greens, watercress, dandelion greens, spring onions and asparagus. To welcome the spring equinox, start plant some seeds indoors or outside if you live in a temperate area, transplant some houseplants, do a spring cleaning of your home (and get rid of clutter), commit to a new healthy habit that brings you joy, donate to a house rabbit adoption agency, make a watercolor painting.

I'm listening to "It Might As Well Be Spring" by Nina Simone.

Summer Solstice

Summer solstice occurs between June 20 - 22 in the Northern Hemisphere and is the lightest, warmest time of the year, and it is technically the first day of summer. The sun is the most enduring symbol of this time of year, along with flowers - especially daisies and sunflowers - dragonflies, butterflies and other emblems of vitality, warmth and life. Reds, oranges, greens and blues can awaken our summer solstice spirit and foods like salads, broccoli, fresh herbs (especially basil, oregano and dill), tomatoes, zucchini, peaches, watermelon, berries, corn, beets, sun tea and much, much more can help you get in summer mode. Playing hopscotch, going on a swing or seesaw, cloud gazing, swimming or splashing in a natural body of water, weaving a daisy or dandelion crown or necklace, running through a sprinkler, setting up a lemonade stand (proceeds to an animal shelter, perhaps?), spending some time barefoot with the cool grass under your feet are all things you can do to pay homage to summer solstice, too.

On my playlist is "Sister Golden Hair," by America.

Autumn Equinox

Falling between September 22 - 24 in the Northern Hemisphere, the autumn equinox is a time of a blast of glorious, vibrant color, fresh, aromatic air, crisper temperatures and an abundance of new produce before things quiet down for winter. Colors in the brown, red, orange, gold, green families can boost your appreciation of the equinox and doing another big house cleaning can feel especially appropriate now but don't forget to leave some chestnuts, acorns and maple leaves out as a cheerful reminder of the season. Foods to enjoy include kale, collards, rosemary, sage, cranberries, apple, pumpkin, sweet potatoes, cinnamon, ciders, breads, nuts and winter squashes. Ring in the equinox by visiting a pumpkin patch, apple orchard or corn maze (find one without petting zoos or other forms of animal exploitation), change your wardrobe to reflect the warmer weather, begin a practice of keeping a gratitude list, host or attend a bonfire with vegan marshmallows, go on a hike or a bike ride in the woods, burn sage to cleanse your home, change out your bedding and furniture coverings to reflect the cooler seasons ahead.

The song to get me in the right mood is "Season of the Witch" by Donovan.

About the Author

Marla Rose is a freelance journalist, columnist, author, recipe developer, public speaker, event planner and mother. After leaving her job in humane education, Marla and her husband John Beske co-founded **VeganStreet.com**. In addition to creating content for Vegan Street, Marla writes the "**Ask Marla**" advice column for *VegNews* magazine. She is co-founder of **Chicago VeganMania**, also with her husband, the biggest free vegan festival in the region. In 2009, Marla and John were awarded the ***Mercy For Animals*** *Activists of the Year* award. They live in the Chicago area with their son, dog and two cats.

VeganStreet.com was originally founded in 1998 and revived after a long hiatus in 2013. With more than a quarter of a million followers on their social media platforms, VeganStreet.com shares new content with the world each week and is most famous for their widely-shared Vegan Street Memes, though it is also home to more than 200 original recipes and dozens of essays, reviews, interviews and vegan living tips. All the content on VeganStreet.com is shared freely with the world, but they do get some much appreciated support from our patrons on **Patreon.com/veganstreet**, and Marla would be thrilled if you decided to become a Patreon patron yourself.

Also by Marla Rose

The Vegan Street Guide for New Vegans

**When Vegans (Almost) Rule the World
and Other Hopeful Projections from the Vegan Feminist Agitator**

The Adventures of Vivian Sharpe, Vegan Superhero

VeganStreet.com

Chase 12/7   770

Cap1 12/8   110.51

         11/30   11.00

Apple

                386.36 Total

HD   12/1   (Aug 1ST is
                  end of promo
                  period)